MW01632312

# SHAKESPEARE'S
## WOMEN IN LOVE

# SHAKESPEARE'S WOMEN IN LOVE

For Patty,
With all best regards,
Alice Griffin

ALICE GRIFFIN

PENTLAND PRESS, INC.
www.pentlandpressusa.com

PUBLISHED BY PENTLAND PRESS, INC.
5122 Bur Oak Circle, Raleigh, North Carolina 27612
United States of America
919-782-0281

ISBN 1-57197-237-4
Library of Congress Control Number: 00-133646



Printed in the United States of America

*To John A. and John B.*

# TABLE OF CONTENTS

# PREFACE

*Love, love, nothing but love, still love, still more!*

—*Troilus and Cressida*, III, i, 109

In all of Shakespeare's comedies and in most of the tragedies, love plays a part. It may lead to happiness or to tragedy for the characters it motivates. It determines both their actions and their language. And for the Elizabethan audience, like today's, Shakespeare's characters solve problems common to that most important relationship between men and women: love.

More than half his plays deal with the courtship of women by men and men by women, lovers of both sexes being tested, marriage and its problems, love woefully going wrong in tragedy and joyfully going right in the comedies. With so much love on the stage, it may be assumed that Shakespeare's audience then as now was captivated by his portrayals of the many aspects of love, from Rosalind wittily testing Orlando in *As You Like It* to Portia in *The Merchant of Venice* covertly declaring her love for Bassanio using a strategy Freud first defined as a "slip."

Just as audiences today are influenced by films and television as well as by theater, so the Elizabethan plays offered women patterns of behavior in their relationships with men. In matters of courtship (a word Shakespeare himself coined), Rosalind in *As You Like It* takes the initiative, making the first approach, as Orlando is smitten but tongue-tied. She goes further: She tests his love with role-playing that protects her own feelings. Both Orlando and the men in *Love's Labour's Lost* use flowery language to declare their love. But is it real love?

As a commuting husband whose family remained in Stratford while he worked in London, Shakespeare well knew that marriage is not an end but a beginning. There is plenty of advice for married women. Portia uses all of her intelligence in *The Merchant of Venice* to vie with his best friend for Bassanio's affection. Which should prevail? Friendship or the marriage? Three of the comedies deal with wives wrongfully accused of infidelity: *Much Ado About Nothing, The Winter's Tale,* and *Cymbeline.* Should she leave, as her husband does, or follow through and prove herself? Helena in *All's Well that Ends Well* wins the husband she wants, only to find that he doesn't want her. Being an intelligent and persistent new woman, she meets the challenge and wins.

Has the wife contributed when tragedy strikes a marriage? Dazzled by Othello's popularity and heroism, Desdemona could not have known him very long or very well before their elopement. Lady Macbeth sublimates her selfhood to help the husband she loves achieve his ambition to be king. When there is a second marriage, where does loyalty lie? In *Hamlet,* Gertrude's heart is "cleft in twain" by her love for both Claudius and Hamlet.

Infidelity can lead to tragedy, as with Regan and Goneril in *King Lear* or to disillusionment, as in *Troilus and Cressida.* Antony leaves two wives for Cleopatra. What are her secrets that make her Shakespeare's most alluring woman?

In matters of love, courtship, and marriage in the comedies, Shakespeare's women are the major players and dominate the action. Women in love in the tragedies may, like Ophelia, be defeated by circumstance; or, like Lady Macbeth, by their decisions; or, like Cleopatra, they may triumph over tragedy.

What a revelation for women (who made up almost half the Elizabethan audience[1])to find in the comedies (which as a genre outnumber the tragedies and the histories) role models who were intelligent and resourceful, who if necessary took the incentive and proposed, who overcame obstacles to achieve a happy union with the man of their choice. Even a woman's choosing her own partner, rather than accepting the mate designated by her father, was new and exciting in Shakespeare's day. With Queen Elizabeth setting the example, education for women was on the increase. The women who decide for themselves in Shakespeare's plays are intelligent and articulate. Analyses of the dialogue of each major female character reveal that it is distinctive and unique to that character, whose delineation her language reinforces. Women use words as a display of wit (like Beatrice), as a defense (like Hermione), and as a logical argument (like Helena). In general, the language of Shakespeare's women is more direct and frank than that of the men, more apt to confess than to conceal weaknesses, and more reliant on vowel sounds for rhythmic and musical effects.

A Shakespeare play takes on an aura of realism when women in love seek advice from their female friends in intimate encounters that are unique in Elizabethan drama. In some nineteen scenes, Shakespeare depicts women alone together in their own world, discussing intimate matters. Such interludes may provide comic sexual innuendo, as in *Much Ado About Nothing*, but Emilia, alone with Desdemona in *Othello*, argues for women's sexual freedom so explicitly that the passage was evidently expurgated from the quarto edition of the play. It appears only in the 1623 folio version, based on the acting text.

In farces like *The Comedy of Errors* and *The Merry Wives of Windsor*, the men are, predictably, extremists, but their wives are realists. In the latter play, Alice and Margaret seek revenge against Falstaff, who has insulted them; in the former, wife Adriana complains to her sister about an unfaithful husband. In the romances, wives accused of infidelity defend themselves, like Hermione, or take action, like Imogen. Deserted by her husband, Helena in *All's Well that Ends Well* pursues and wins him through intelligence and persistence.

Although Shakespeare solves some marriage problems, he seems satisfied merely to depict others, leaving judgment to the audience. Mutual respect in marriage has a high priority as a solution in plays as different as *The Taming of the Shrew* and *Julius Caesar*. In the latter, the mutuality of Portia and Brutus is contrasted to the strained relationship of Calphurnia and Caesar.

Shakespeare confines extramarital relationships to historical characters. The unfaithful Queen Margaret carries on an affair with Suffolk; despises her dysfunctional husband, Henry VI; seizes his leadership role; and takes on its worst characteristics. Goneril and Regan, daughters of Britain's King Lear, self-destruct over their infatuation for Edmund. From classical history Shakespeare draws the two most famous legendary pairs of lovers: Helen and Paris and Antony and Cleopatra. The glamour goes sour in his antiheroic depiction of Helen and Paris in *Troilus and Cressida*, but Cleopatra in her "infinite variety" is the epitome of an alluring woman in a mature relationship.

In hopes that this volume will contribute to the understanding of Shakespeare's women by students, teachers, and general readers/theatergoers, I analyze character and language in conjunction with action. In the relevant quotations from the text, spelling is modernized, and archaic words explained at the foot of the page. As Shakespeare wrote for the ear, not for the eye, punctuation in the quoted text is light, based on the early quartos and on the First Folio. Some of the early quartos are believed to be close to Shakespeare's original manuscript, available to a printer once a scribe made a "fair copy" for the playhouse. The First Folio of 1623 was compiled from the first acting scripts. From the quartos and folio, I also restore original wording emended by later editors. For my consultation of these early texts I thank the British Library. When a final "ed" is to be pronounced so that a line of iambic verse scans, it is marked 'e. References to act, scene, and line are from the Arden edition.

Mindful that Shakespeare wrote for performance, I refer to recent films, to stage productions, and to the television series issued by the British Broadcasting Corporation in association with Time-Life, currently in school and university libraries throughout the United States and the United Kingdom and comprising the only record of visual performance of the complete canon. In this respect, I am grateful to the American Council of Learned Societies for their support.

I thank my colleagues and students at Lehman College of The City University of New York for their helpful suggestions as I worked over a period of years on this endeavor to evaluate commonly held interpretations and to present new points of view about Shakespeare's women in love.

## Notes

[1] Alfred Harbage, *Shakespeare's Audience*, 74–78.

# SECTION 1.

## LOVE AND COURTSHIP

"The course of true love never did run smooth," observes Lysander in *A Midsummer Night's Dream* to Hermia, who is threatened with death unless she marries her father's choice. As they elaborate, it is the theme of all Shakespeare's comedies and one tragedy treating love and courtship. (I, i, 134–42)

Lysander: *But either it was different in blood—*
Hermia: *O cross! Too high to be enthralled to low,*

—*The Winter's Tale*

Lysander: *Or else it stood upon the choice of friends*[i]*—*
Hermia: *O hell! To choose love by another's eyes.*

—*A Midsummer Night's Dream*

Lysander: *Or if there were a sympathy in choice*
*War, death, or sickness did lay siege to it.*

—*Romeo and Juliet*

[i] relatives

# CHAPTER ONE: EARLY COMEDIES

*Love's Labour's Lost, A Midsummer Night's Dream, The Two Gentlemen of Verona,* and *The Merchant of Venice*

*Love's Labour's Lost*—The Princess of France, Rosaline, Maria, Katherine

In Shakespeare's early, mature, and late comedies, women dominate. Although fewer in number, female characters stand out as individuals, but the men who woo them or whom they woo barely can be distinguished one from the other. In *Love's Labour's Lost,* a group of women confront and solve one of the problems of love: how to test whether the man's love is sincere or whether he is merely exercising a stereotypical approach in imitation of his peers. The plot is simple and probably original with Shakespeare: The King of Navarre and three companions decide to withdraw from the world and study in a "little academe," a men's campus where women are not welcome or even permitted within miles of the place. Four women arrive on the scene; the Princess of France, attended by three ladies-in-waiting, is calling on the king on state business on behalf of her father. Predictably, the two leaders fall in love, as do the other three pairs of men and women.

Filled with verse and musical dialogue, the action is patterned like a love ballet. The men declare their love, are tested and found wanting, and finally are instructed to leave their academe and live in the real world before the women will make a commitment. The very artificiality of the action throws into relief the real concern at its heart—choosing the right marriage partner. From the master at creating and understanding human behavior there are lessons to be learned.

As the play opens, that the men agree to such extreme measures is a matter of peer pressure, of following suit. The one realistic member of the quartet, Berowne, points out that their vow to withdraw from normal life will be impossible to keep: "O these are barren tasks, too hard to keep, / Not to see ladies, study, fast, not sleep" (I, i, 47–48).

Nevertheless, unwilling to be the outsider, he joins them in their decision. As soon as the women appear, all vows are forgotten, and each man composes a love sonnet to the lady of his choice, who just happens to fancy him, too. The very artificiality of their verse sounds a warning to the women, as do the presents or favors each receives from her would-be lover. The men's verses, with forced rhymes and well-worn imagery, could be from model-letter books popular then. As for the gifts, they prove useful in a test devised by the women.

Together in one of the "women's world" scenes that recur in the comedies, amid bawdy talk, they decide to exchange among themselves the gifts that were intended to identify them in a forthcoming masquerade. The men, disguised as Russians, appear in a masque, a formal song-and-dance presentation, and seek out the masked women, each wearing her identifying (but exchanged) gift. The test will prove whether each man really knows the woman to whom he has been swearing eternal love. Or is their declared love so shallow that it is based on externals? What follows is a comedy of mistaken identity, of farcical goings-on that end in a compromise.

Berowne is the wittiest of the men, and Rosaline is the brightest of the women, as their banter displays when the masquerade is exposed:

> Berowne: *your capacity*
> *Is of that nature that to your huge store*
> *Wise things seem foolish, and rich things but poor.*
> Rosaline: *This proves you wise and rich, for in my eye—*
> Berowne: *I am a fool, and full of poverty.* (V, ii, 376–80)

He renounces the overblown style of his love declarations:

> *O never will I trust to speeches penned,*
> *Nor to the motion of a schoolboy's tongue. . . .*
> *Henceforth my wooing mind shall be expressed*

*In russet yeas and honest kersey*[i]*noes.*
*And to begin, wench, so God help me law,*
*My love to thee is sound, sans crack or flaw.*
Rosaline: *Sans "sans," I pray you.* (V, ii, 402–16)

Likewise, each of the other men sees the error of his earlier, rhetorical attempts at wooing and in a straightforward manner declares his love for his chosen woman. The men recognize as extreme and unnatural their earlier strictures against women entering their domain and invite the women to leave their dwelling in the fields to reside at the king's court. The women reject the invitation, reminding the men of their previous too-hasty oath.

Suddenly, reality intrudes with the news of the death of the princess's father, and the women must leave. The men attempt to press them for a commitment before departing: "Now at the latest minute of the hour / Grant us your loves," asks the king. Knowing that a waiting period will only strengthen real love, the princess replies rationally to their urge to commit immediately: "A time methinks too short, / To make a world-without-end bargain in" (V, ii, 781-83).

Instead, the women will announce their decisions in a year and a day. Suggesting that the men use the year usefully in the world, not withdrawn from it, the princess sends Navarre to a hermitage:

*If this austere insociable life*
*Change not your offer made in heat of blood,*
*If frosts and fasts, hard lodging and thin weeds*[ii]
*Nip not the gaudy blossoms of your love,*
*But that it bear this trial, and last*[iii] *love,*
*Then at the expiration of the year . . .*
*I will be thine.* (V, ii, 793-801)

Rosaline directs Berowne, who criticizes the world with no real knowledge of it, to address his jests and "idle scorns" to "the speechless sick" in hospitals to see if they will listen:

*But if they will not, throw away that spirit,*
*And I shall find you empty of that fault,*
*Right joyful of your reformation.* (V, ii, 855-57)

[i] coarse cloth [ii] clothing [iii] that is, last as

Dumaine is instructed by Katherine to grow a beard and live chaste, Longaville by Maria to grow older and presumably more experienced. Although Berowne complains that "Our wooing doth not end like an old play: / Jack hath not Jill," Navarre, who is learning patience, reminds him that it will end in a year and a day. Berowne: "That's too long for a play" (V, ii, 862-66).

Like *A Midsummer Night's Dream*, the play ends with a "show" staged by the local citizens for the entertainment of royalty. This likely reflects actual practice, when Queen Elizabeth witnessed such shows as she went on "progress" through the countryside.[1] As did Queen Elizabeth, the princess displays enormous patience at the amateur show of the Nine Worthies enacted by the townspeople. Her kind remarks to them are in contrast to the behavior of the men. Led by Berowne, they are loudly critical of the bumbling efforts of the curate, the schoolmaster, the constable, the rustic Costard, and the little page, all wildly inappropriate for their roles, enacting biblical and historical "worthies" or heroes.

In two final songs at the end, Shakespeare demonstrates his versatility in writing every type of verse and doing it better than anyone else. Throwing into relief the decorative, sparkling, witty dialogue of the courtiers, come two beautiful lyrics in the simple language Rosaline recommended to Berowne. The cuckoo and the owl sing, representing spring and winter. First spring sings of that season:

*When daisies pied and violets blue,*
*And lady-smocks all silver-white,*
*And cuckoo-buds of yellow hue,*
*Do paint the meadows with delight,*
*The cuckoo then on every tree*
*Mocks married men.*

Then winter sings :

*When icicles hang by the wall,*
*And Dick the shepherd blows his nail,*
*And Tom bears logs into the hall,*
*And milk comes frozen home in pail,*
*When blood is nipped, and ways be foul,*
*Then nightly sings the staring owl.* (V, ii, 882-87; 900-5)

The lyric, pictorial evocation of the changing seasons and passing time returns to the opening lines. Then Navarre spoke of "cormorant devouring Time," hoping, through withdrawal from the world to "bate[i] his scythe's keen edge." Now, with love to inspire them, and directed by the women, the men will return to the world with its beauty and rigors depicted in the closing lyrics and, in time, prove their love.

The BBC Time-Life television production of this play is notable for its setting in the eighteenth century, when academies flourished, and for its posing of the women, like paintings by Fragonard, in their scenes together. Jonathan Kent as the king and Maureen Lipman as the princess are impressive, delivering their lines with clarity and conviction.

*A Midsummer Night's Dream*—Hermia and Helena

"Reason and love," says Bottom in *A Midsummer Night's Dream*, "keep little company together nowadays" (III, i, 137-38). Although he is wearing an ass's head at the time, he aptly expresses the behavior governing the young lovers as it does in real life. As Lysander himself points out, he and Demetrius are indistinguishable one from the other; Helena and Hermia are differentiated mainly in appearance. In the throes of love all act irrationally, yet by the end of the night in the magical forest, true love prevails. The play resembles *Love's Labour's Lost* in that both have original plots that deal with love between multiple couples, and both end with shows performed before royalty, suggesting that the works themselves may have been presented to celebrate a royal occasion. The characters of the women in *Dream* are more fully delineated: suffering as the play opens, then surmounting obstacles and ending happily with the men of their choice. Although they have been friends since childhood, sexual jealousy makes them enemies temporarily.

Hermia is under a threat of death unless she renounce her loved one, Lysander, and marry her father's choice, Demetrius. Refusing to accept the patriarchal decision, she and Lysander decide to elope through the forest to a sympathetic aunt. They share the news of the planned elopement with Helena, who, in an attempt to win back the affection of Demetrius, asks Hermia

[i] abate

what means she employs to make Demetrius love her. Helena believes she lost him because of her appearance and that looking like Hermia might recapture his love:

*Sickness is catching: O were favour*[i] *so,*
*Yours would I catch, fair Hermia, ere I go,*
*My ear should catch your voice, my eye your eye,*
*My tongue should catch your tongue's sweet melody.*
*Were the world mine, Demetrius being bated,*[ii]
*The rest I'ld give to be to you translated.*[iii]
*O teach me how you look, and with what art*
*You sway the motion of Demetrius' heart.* (I, i, 186–93)

Transformation will be one of the themes of the play, for in the moonlight forest all four young lovers will be transformed after experiencing a veritable seesaw of emotions. Under the influence of Puck's magic flower, both men will switch their affections from Hermia to Helena, while Hermia—basing her argument on appearance—blames Helena, and the two formerly devoted friends now almost come to blows:

*Now I perceive that she hath made compare*
*Between our statures, she hath urged her height,*
*And with her personage, her tall personage,*
*Her height (forsooth) she hath prevailed with him.*
*And are you grown so high in his esteem,*
*Because I am so dwarfish and so low?*
*How low am I, thou painted maypole?* (III, ii, 290–96)

Although the women are not greatly differentiated from each other, they are very different from the two men both in their language and in their constancy. The speech of the men, especially in expressing their newly discovered love for Helena, is rhetorical, much of it in rhyme, like the love declarations in *Love's Labour's Lost*. The women are simple and down to earth in their expression; much of it is monosyllabic. This style lends poignancy to Hermia's plight when she cannot believe that Lysander has lost his love for her in the course of the night:

*Am not I Hermia? Are not you Lysander?*
*I am as fair now, as I was erewhile.*

[i] appearance [ii] subtracted, excepted [iii] transformed

*Since night, you loved me; yet since night, you left me.*
(III, ii, 273–75)

The men change and then change back under the influence of magic juice, but the women remain constant in their loves, Hermia for Lysander and Helena for Demetrius, who after the night in the woods explains his change of heart to Duke Theseus:

*my love to Hermia,*
*Melted as the snow, seems to me now*
*As the remembrance of an idle gaud,*[i]
*Which in my childhood I did dote upon:*
*And all the faith, the virtue of my heart,*
*The object and the pleasure of mine eye,*
*Is only Helena.* (IV, i, 164–70)

Bottom believes that reason and love might be made compatible by some "honest neighbor." Theseus, in the play's most philosophical passage, takes the opposite view: Lovers, like lunatics and poets (Shakespeare includes himself in the group), are "of imagination all compact," and thus they "apprehend / More than cool reason ever comprehends" (V, i, 5–8). As "the course of true love never did run smooth" (I, i, 134), the four have been on an emotional roller coaster of misunderstandings, jealousy, and verbal assaults. But with the help of love's magic juice, they have survived the night and its dangers, for love gives them a special understanding ("apprehension") that may go beyond what reason can grasp.

After their journey through the magic woods, they awake from their sleep and decide on their future. Theseus announces that he and Hippolyta and the two young couples will "eternally be knit" (180). In celebration of the marriages, the tradesmen's "tedious brief scene" of Pyramus and Thisby is an unintentional burlesque of the love and death of legendary lovers, similar to the show of Nine Worthies in *Love's Labour's Lost*. The play ends with a final blessing on the married pairs by a song and dance of fairies, led by Titania and Oberon, who sings:

*To the best bride-bed will we,*
*Which by us shall blesse'd be:*
*And the issue*[ii] *there create,*
*Ever shall be fortunate:*

[i] toy [ii] children

*So shall all the couples three*
*Ever true in loving be.* (V, i, 389-94)

The 1935 black-and-white film of the Max Reinhardt production of *A Midsummer Night's Dream* still has much to recommend it. Reinhardt's acclaimed German production was reproduced in the Hollywood Bowl, after which it was filmed. The visual effect, set to Mendelssohn's music, is magical, shot through with stars and moonlight, and with troupes of children as the fairies. The actors are varied, from Dick Powell "hamming" the role of Lysander, to Olivia de Havilland, a sympathetic and clearly articulate Hermia. James Cagney is surprisingly effective as Bottom, and Joe E. Brown a treasure as Flute enacting Thisby. The 1968 BBC television production directed by Peter Hall and set in the 1960s starred Judi Dench as a scantily clad Titania and Diana Rigg as a Mary Quant mini-skirted Helena. Peter Brook's production at the London National Theatre is best remembered for Oberon and Titania swinging on trapeze bars.

*The Two Gentlemen of Verona*—Julia and Sylvia

Like *A Midsummer Night's Dream, The Two Gentlemen of Verona* is concerned with men changing their affections; there is no magic juice, so the suggestion is that this is an all-too-human condition. The play contrasts the steadfast love of Julia, an appealing yet weak heroine, with the lightly motivated, changeable affection of her lover, Proteus. In a love relationship, a woman then as now might feel threatened by her partner's friendship with another man, not to mention that partner's infatuation with his friend's loved one. In the spirit of mutual affection, both men readily hand over the woman they say they love to their friend. Here, with a heroine who is too accepting, male friendship prevails over love, a conflict Shakespeare presents again, with different results, in *The Merchant of Venice*. Like the shape-changing sea god for whom he is named, Proteus is inconstant. Leaving Verona for Milan, where his friend Valentine has gone, Proteus swears undying love for Julia, who believes him and decides to follow him.

For the journey, she will disguise herself as a page boy to "prevent / The loose encounters of lascivious men" (II, vii,

40–41). Her more rational friend Lucetta suggests that waiting for Proteus's return might be preferable to pursuit. Reason versus emotion in love is again a theme as it was in *A Midsummer Night's Dream*. In a speech that is plain and direct in contrast to Julia's hyperbole, Lucetta tries to "qualify" the "hot fire" of Julia's love, "Lest it should burn above the bounds of reason," but Julia replies, "The more thou damm'st it up, the more it burns" (21-24). When Julia insists that Proteus's declarations of love, his "thousand oaths, an ocean of his tears," assure her of a warm welcome from him, Lucetta reminds her: "All these are servants to deceitful men." Julia invokes the universe in her confidence that Proteus is different: "His heart as far from fraud, as heaven from earth," to which the more down-to-earth Lucetta replies, "Pray heaven he prove so when you come to him" (69–72; 78–79).

In Milan, as soon as Proteus sees Valentine's inamorata, Sylvia, he falls in love with her and renounces his friendship: "Methinks my zeal to Valentine is cold, / And that I love him not as I was wont" (II, iv, 199–200). When Proteus sues to Sylvia for her love, she doubts his sincerity and reminds him of his earlier suit to Julia. Sylvia's plain, outspoken style will become characteristic of Shakespeare's women who speak their minds, like Paulina in *The Winter's Tale*. Sylvia verbally attacks Proteus:

*Thou subtle, perjured, false disloyal man:*
*Think'st thou I am so shallow, so conceitless*[i]
*To be seduc'ed by thy flattery,*
*That hast deceived so many with thy vows?* (IV, ii, 92–95)

Suffering in her page's disguise, Julia is forced to act as Proteus's emissary when he hires her to carry her own ring to his new love, Sylvia, who again berates Proteus:

*The more shame for him that he sends it me;*
*For I have heard him say a thousand times,*
*His Julia gave it him at his departure:*
*Though his false finger have profaned the ring,*
*Mine shall not do his Julia so much wrong.* (IV, iv, 131–35)

Instead of regarding herself as a rival to Julia, Sylvia shows sympathetic understanding. In a lyric passage, at Sylvia's

[i] unimaginative

questioning, pageboy Julia mirrors her own plight as she describes how in a pageant "he" played "the woman's part," that of Ariadne deserted by Theseus:

*I did play a lamentable part,*
*Madam, 'twas Ariadne passioning*
*For Theseus' perjury and unjust flight.* (IV, iv, 164-66)

The description has a similar effect on Sylvia: "Alas, poor lady, desolate and left; / I weep myself to think upon thy words" (IV, iv, 172–73).

When Proteus again declares his love for Sylvia, she reminds him of the mutual love between her and Valentine. Sylvia says nothing at all when Valentine gives her to Proteus, nor when she is handed back to Valentine. Presumably, she still loves him. When Julia's disguise is revealed, Proteus, in a further shift of heart, decides that he loves her after all. Apologizing for her disguise, Julia compares her change of costume to his change of mind: "It is the lesser blot, modesty finds, / Women to change their shapes than men their minds." Proteus's self-satisfied reply is characteristic of him:

*Than men their minds? 'tis true. O heaven, were man*
*But constant, he were perfect; that one error*
*Fills him with faults; makes him run through all th' sins:*
*Inconstancy falls off ere it begins.*
*What is in Silvia's face, but I may spy*
*More fresh in Julia's with a constant eye?* (V, iv, 107–14)

That Proteus has learned a lesson and will prove to have a "constant eye" is to be hoped. But there is something unsatisfying in the conclusion, which might be acceptable in prose (the plot derives from Montemayor's *Diana* and is used by Cervantes as well), but on the stage, acted by real people, it does not work. Shakespeare was to find a better solution to the theme of love versus friendship in *The Merchant of Venice* through Portia, the first of his well-rounded, individual, gifted heroines.

### *The Merchant of Venice*—Portia

The challenge faced by Portia in *The Merchant of Venice* is not uncommon among women: For her husband's affections, she must vie with his best friend. She will muster all her intelligence and understanding to combat the strong tie between Antonio, the merchant, and her beloved Bassanio. In the past Antonio has financed the seemingly idle younger man who has, he admits, squandered the money. As the play opens, Bassanio comes to the merchant with a sure-fire proposal for a return on his investment: "In Belmont is a lady richly left" (I, i, 161). In addition to the riches of her inheritance, the lady once gave him encouraging glances. If Bassanio had the means to outfit himself splendidly like her other suitors, he tells his friend, there is no doubt he would "be fortunate."[i] Although Antonio's ships are all at sea, he will borrow the needed money from Shylock, a money-lender who will not take interest, but "in a merry sport" a pound of Antonio's flesh to be forfeit if the debt is not repaid.

Promising to return with speed, Bassanio sets sail for Belmont. The parting is difficult for Antonio, who displays a tactic he obviously has employed in the past and will continue to use with Bassanio: by being generous and saying he expects nothing in return, he instills guilt in Bassanio for taking rather than giving. Antonio tells Bassanio to stay as long as he likes and not even think about the bond (but hoping that he will). Friend Salerio describes Antonio's parting from his young friend:

*And even there, his eye being big with tears,*
*Turning his face, he put his hand behind him,*
*And with affection wondrous sensible*
*He wrung Bassanio's hand, and so they parted.* (II, viii, 46–49)

To this Salanio responds: "I think he only loves the world for him" (50).

As soon as Portia makes her first appearance, discussing her many suitors with her attendant, Nerissa, the audience is aware that she is an unusual woman. The balanced prose she speaks signifies intelligence; the internal rhyme suggests liveliness and imagination on her part:

> *This reasoning is not in the fashion to choose me a husband. O me, the word "choose." I may neither choose who I would, nor refuse who I dislike, so is the will of a living daughter curbed by the will of a dead father: is it not hard Nerissa, that I cannot choose one, nor refuse none?*
> (I, ii, 20–26)

[i] (a) be lucky (b) acquire a fortune

Nerissa responds that Portia's father "was ever virtuous," and that his scheme for suitors to choose from three caskets of gold, silver, and lead would guarantee that the one who chooses "rightly" also will be "one who you shall rightly love" (30–31). Shakespeare is having it both ways here: a woman's right to choose her own husband, as against parental choice, was a current topic of debate. In this case, says Nerissa, the father's choice and Portia's are fated to agree.

But Portia is not quite content to leave all to fate when it comes to Bassanio's choosing. He has arrived in style with "gifts of rich value" after a prince and a king have chosen, wrongly, the caskets of gold and silver. Before Bassanio begins his choice, Portia tries to persuade him to prolong his visit:

*for in choosing wrong*
*I lose your company; therefore forbear a while,*
*There's something tells me—but it is not love—*
*I would not lose you.* (III, ii, 2–5)

She is advancing and retreating, saying and unsaying that she loves him. Her now-famous Freudian slip hints at her love, withdraws it, offers it again:

*One half of me is yours, the other half yours,—*
*Mine own I would say: but if mine then yours,*
*And so all yours.* (III, ii, 16–18)

He is not ready to trust to fate either, and asks for a hint: "O happy torment, when my torturer / Doth teach me answers for deliverance" (36–37). She "teaches" him two "answers": her statement "I stand for sacrifice" (57) and then a song in which the line-end words rhyme with "lead":

*Tell me where is Fancy bred,*
*Or in the heart, or in the head?*
*How begot, how nourish'ed?* (III, ii, 63–65)

Despite his earlier need of a loan to achieve a splendid appearance, which he believed guaranteed a favorable impression, Bassanio gets the message: "So may the outward shows be least themselves, / The world is still deceived with ornament" (III, ii, 73–74) and correctly chooses the lead casket. Not only had the "outward show" been important to him as a suitor, but it continues to be so, as he now praises not Portia's beauty but that of her portrait found in the casket. Then he kisses her, and "giddy" with love, is not too giddy to ask that all be "confirmed, signed, ratified by you" (III, ii, 148).

Another mark of Portia's ability to think quickly is reflected in her dialogue here, as she picks up and develops his metaphor drawn from business. She wishes that her "virtues, beauties, livings, friends" might "exceed account." At the same time, she is aware of the need to appear modest lest she reveal merits that exceed his. She says that the "sum" of her, to "term in gross, / Is an unlessoned girl, unschooled, unpracticed" (160), yet willing to learn. She turns over everything to him: "This house, these servants, and this same myself," symbolized by a ring she places on his finger,

*Which when you part from, lose, or give away,*
*Let it presage the ruin of your love,*
*And be my vantage*[i] *to exclaim on you.* (III, ii, 170–74)

The ring is not a device to keep the plot running once the trial scene is resolved, as some earlier critics have charged, but rather it is integral to the Portia-Bassanio-Antonio triangle.[2]

Divested of the household management and of the tensions of the ceremonial choice of casket, Portia seems to enjoy a new freedom and an opportunity to display considerable versatility. Now that she has won Bassanio, she will need all of her resources to hold him. Bassanio evidently has not thought of Antonio since they bade farewell in Venice, but now, at the moment of celebration, the merchant's letter arrives; it will defer consummation of the marriage. The tone of the letter is in keeping with Antonio's earlier dealings with Bassanio, who must feel guilty because the older man's generosity that financed the courtship has now rebounded and threatens his very life: "[As] it is impossible I should live, all debts are cleared between you and I, if I might but see you at my death . . . If your love do not persuade you to come, let not my letter" (III, ii, 316–20).

Portia asks, "Is it your dear friend that is thus in trouble?" and Bassanio replies, "The dearest friend to me, the kindest man, / The best-conditioned and unwearied spirit / In doing courtesies" (290–93). Portia's response, of many she might make,

[i] opportunity

again reveals her quick thinking. If Antonio is generous, she can outdo him in generosity: a boundless sum to be offered to Shylock, and immediately after their marriage ceremony, Bassanio is to leave for Venice (another shrewd move, to put off consummation until he returns):

> *Pay him six thousand, and deface the bond:*
> *Double six thousand, and then treble that,*
> *Before a friend of this description*
> *Shall lose a hair through Bassanio's fault. . . .*
> *For never shall you lie by Portia's side*
> *With an unquiet soul. You shall have gold*
> *To pay the petty debt twenty times over.*
> *When it is paid, bring your true friend along.* (III, ii, 298–307)

Not only does her generosity out-Antonio Antonio, but also she cleverly invites him back to Belmont, so that she can judge the competition and so that Bassanio may compare them in person. The clarity of this statement reveals her logical mind. No longer is Portia using decorative prose, as when she describes her suitors to Nerissa, or verse that strikes a delicate balance between revealing and concealing her love for Bassanio. Her character is developed in words as well as action; the logic of this passage prepares the audience for her courtroom defense of Antonio.

Armed with notes and suitable clothing from her cousin Bellario, a distinguished doctor of law, Portia embarks on a display of generosity prompted by the mutuality of their marriage. She has told Bassanio, "I am half yourself," and if Bassanio values Antonio, she must save him. Their mutual happiness depends on the success of her defense of Antonio, whose martyrdom would cast a permanent shadow over the marriage, including the marriage bed. If she succeeds in the court, outdoing Antonio both in generosity and in loyalty, she may be able to demonstrate to Bassanio that marriage takes precedence over male friendship.

Even with Bellario's notes and his recommendation of her to the court as "a young doctor of Rome" named Balthazar, Portia faces a trial of her own. But intelligence and eloquence are on her side. The best-known passage of the play, the "quality of mercy speech" addressed to Shylock and urging mercy rather than strict justice, is musical in its use of light, short vowels contrasted with open, long diphthongs, which are repeated, like "rain" and "strain," while the repetition of the "s" sound in "mercy" and "sceptred sway" (189) and "likest God's / When mercy seasons justice" (192–93) suggests the sound of waters, a constant image in this play set in Venice. (Musical effect is one of the ways Shakespeare distinguishes women's speeches from men's.) The progression of thought is rational, moving from heaven to earth, from the metaphor of rain, which like mercy, comes from heaven, to an example of mercy on earth, in kings as "an attribute to God himself," and then back to heaven and God's mercy on all:

*The quality of mercy is not strained,*
*It droppeth as the gentle rain from heaven*
*Upon the place beneath: it is twice blest,*
*It blesseth him that gives, and him that takes,*
*'Tis mightiest in the mightiest, it becomes*
*The thron'ed monarch better than his crown.*
*His sceptre shows the force of temporal power,*
*The attribute to awe and majesty,*
*Wherein doth sit the dread and fear of kings:*
*But mercy is above this sceptred sway,*
*It is enthron'ed in the hearts of kings,*
*It is an attribute to God himself;*
*And earthly power doth then show likest God's*
*When mercy seasons justice.* (IV, i, 180–93)

Unmoved, Shylock insists on justice and calls for judgment. Portia asks Antonio if he has any last words. He has quite a few. He takes Bassanio's hand and bids him an emotional farewell, imploring that Bassanio "Grieve not that I am fallen to this for you," but expecting him to do just that and rubbing in the guilt. He sends greetings to Bassanio's wife:

*Tell her the process of Antonio's end.*
*Say how I loved you, speak me fair in death:*
*And when the tale is told, bid her be judge*
*Whether Bassanio had not once a love:*
*Repent but you that you shall lose your friend*
*And he repents not that he pays your debt.* (IV, i, 270–75)

Antonio's giveaway word here is "once." He does not recognize love between Bassanio and Portia. And the "debt" has been shifted from Antonio to Bassanio. The speech has its desired effect on Bassanio, who pledges that he would give "life itself, my wife, and all the world" to free Antonio. "Your wife would give you little thanks for that / If she were by to hear you make the offer," Portia/Balthazar comments dryly (280, 284–85).

Portia saves Antonio by citing a provision of the law evidently overlooked by all the "learned doctors" in attendance: Shylock may take his pound of flesh but while doing so if he sheds "one drop of Christian blood, [his] lands and goods / Are by the laws of Venice confiscate / Unto the state" (305–308). After Shylock departs, disgraced and disenfranchised, Bassanio and Antonio thank Portia/Balthazar and offer her/him the 3,000 ducats she herself sent to redeem the debt. Portia declines, asking only for Bassanio's ring—the same ring she gave him when they married, commanding him never to part with it. After Bassanio refuses three times, Antonio urges his friend to "let him have the ring, / Let his deservings and my love withal / Be valued 'gainst your wife's commandment" (445–47). In the contest for Bassanio's heart between Antonio's "love withall" and his "wife's commandment," Antonio seems to have won this round. But Portia is looking ahead.

The final scene in moon-drenched, romantic Belmont soon turns to a realistic aspect of marriage—disagreement and misunderstanding. In measured, balanced verse, Bassanio defends his gift of the ring to a "civil doctor," for his honor was at stake: "My honor would not let ingratitude / So much besmear it" (218–19). Using a device other Shakespearean women will employ to advantage, Portia repeats his cadence and his words incrementally to convey an opposite meaning, concluding that he gave the ring to a woman. Both, of course, are right. She threatens him with the same infidelity, she says, he has displayed: "I will become as liberal[i] as you. . . . I'll have that doctor for my bedfellow" (226, 233). (The question of the double standard in sexual infidelity will be discussed more seriously by Emilia in *Othello*.) When Bassanio again vows his fidelity and swears by his soul, Antonio joins in and pledges his soul as surety for Bassanio, as once he pledged his body. Portia hands the original ring to Antonio for delivery to Bassanio and

[i] licentious

produces her cousin Bellario's letter explaining that "Portia was the doctor" (269). Antonio's handing over the ring, which symbolizes marriage, is indicative that marriage has triumphed.

## Notes

[1] Alice Griffin, *Pageantry on the Shakespearean Stage*, 158–61.

[2] Coppelia Kahn, "The Cuckoo's Note," in *Shakespeare's Comedies*, ed. Gary Waller, 132.

# CHAPTER TWO: MATURE COMEDIES

*Twelfth Night*, *As You Like It*, and *Much Ado About Nothing*

*Twelfth Night*—Viola

*Twelfth Night* considers another aspect of women in love: how to win the man you love when he regards you as a friend. Shakespeare bases his main plot on a story by Barnabe Riche.[1] Shipwrecked, Viola calls on her resources, disguises herself as a page called Cesario, and finds employment at the court of Duke Orsino. She immediately falls in love with the duke, but can do nothing about it, especially as he regards her as a younger male friend who needs guidance; he sends her as an emissary to the woman he loves, Olivia. To complete the circle, Olivia, who disdains Orsino's overtures, falls in love with the boy she believes Viola to be.

In addition to resourcefulness, another virtue Viola displays is patience. When Olivia sends Viola a ring, thus taking the initiative (as do Shakespeare's women in love), Viola shrewdly guesses the meaning of the gift and sympathizes with the misplaced love: "Poor lady, she were better love a dream" (II, ii, 25). Then, wisely, she decides to patiently await the solution that will come over time: "O Time, thou must untangle this, not I, / It is too hard a knot for me t'untie (II, ii, 39–40). On the other hand, as Viola well realizes, waiting too long has its drawbacks. In act two, scene four, Orsino and Cesario/Viola have a "man-to-man" discussion about love, with the older man offering advice. C. L. Barber suggests that "the woman who is present there, behind Cesario's disguise, is brought to mind repeatedly by the talk of love and of the differences of men and women in love."[2] Viola finds some relief for her concealed passion by going as far as she can without giving herself away. In answer to Orsino's questions, she confesses loving someone who looks like Orsino and who is about his age. "Let thy love be younger than thyself," advises Orsino, for women's looks, he says, fade quickly. Viola needs no reminder that time may be an enemy as well as a friend. When Orsino brags that no woman can love as deeply as a man, Viola disagrees and tells the story of her father's daughter, relieving her own distress and demonstrating the musicality expected of her. (She declared this talent in her first scene, stating "I can speak to him in many sorts of music.")

*she never told her love,*
*But let concealment like a worm i' th' bud*
*Feed on her damask cheek: she pined in thought,*
*And with a green and yellow melancholy,*
*She sat like Patience on a monument,*
*Smiling at grief.* (II, iv, 111–16)

Patience is personified here as a seated figure carved on a monument, smiling because she knows that patience can alleviate the grief of the mourners. The musical quality of these lines is derived from the repetition of "l" sounds in pairs of words, such as "concealment like" and "yellow melancholy." Assonance adds to the musical effect, with repetition of long, open vowel sounds: "pined," "like," "smiling." The "s" alliteration in "She sat . . . Smiling" leads up to the final long diphthong, stretched out "grief" but also presenting a surprising paradox to the word "smiling."

For this scene and others in which Orsino is confiding in a page he believes to be a boy but who the audience knows is a woman, director Trevor Nunn in the 1996 film placed his faith in young, talented actors. Toby Stephens convincingly demonstrates that Orsino's affection for Viola/Cesario is one of friendship, while Imogen Stubbs as Viola delicately conveys the love she feels for Orsino when they are together. Helena Bonham Carter's impetuosity as Olivia provides a contrast to Viola's patience.

With the intelligence that characterizes all of Shakespeare's major heroines, Viola has another reason to hope that her love for Orsino may one day be realized. She suspects, as does the audience, that Orsino's suit to Olivia will be unsuccessful, because Olivia's affections are directed elsewhere—at Viola as Cesario. That, too, will right itself as soon as Viola's twin brother Sebastian, introduced early in the play, appears in the final scene to the assembled company. He enters just as Orsino—jealous of Olivia's love for Cesario, which has led her to plight her troth to twin Sebastian—threatens Viola's life. Olivia had misplaced her affections on a "maid," says Sebastian. "But nature to her bias drew in that" (258). "Nature," explain the Arden editors, "followed its inborn tendency ['bias'] to mate female with male."[3]

Orsino's love has been misdirected, too, as he finally realizes that Olivia is a cold "marble-breasted tyrant," and turns to the companion he has regarded affectionately for three months:

> *Boy, thou has said to me a thousand times,*
> *Thou never shouldst love woman like to me.*
> Viola: *And all those sayings will I over-swear . . .* (V, i, 265–67)

"He discovers in the page the woman's love he could not win from the countess," comments Barber, who sees the denouement as "the moment when delusions and misapprehensions are resolved by the finding of objects appropriate to passions."[4]

Alone and by her own wits, Viola has survived shipwreck, lowly employment, insults, and threats of bodily injury and of death. Her reward is the man she loves, transformed from a self-indulgent wooer of an unattainable woman to a partner who values her accomplishments and who promises her mutuality in their marriage.

### *As You Like It*—Rosalind and Celia

In *As You Like It*, Rosalind tests the love of Orlando by role-playing. Her position is an enviable one in that it involves no commitment on her part while she plays the "saucy lackey" with him, but it has its risks, too. The position she takes—denigrating his love verses as well as women in general—may be too successful and really "cure" him of love as she proposes to do in the guise of Ganymede. That he may survive her test and emerge with a stronger and more realistic love for her—or he may not—accounts for a tension in Rosalind, who is not all clever lines and boyish strutting but a woman deeply and desperately in love, as actress Juliet Stevenson demonstrated in the role.

Like many a film today, *As You Like It* is based on a best-selling novel, Thomas Lodge's *Rosalynde.* Written in stylized prose, it centers on Rosalynde who, disguised as a boy, meets her lover, Rosader, in the forest, where she tests his love by playing the part of his loved one in a game she devises to cure him of what she insists is only an infatuation.[5]

Inheriting this witty, take-charge heroine, Shakespeare needed to depict the woman beneath the guise she assumes to convince the audience that behind her put-downs of Orlando there is a real and vulnerable love seeking assurance that the love is mutual. Resourceful and realistic, Rosalind is a Shakespearean heroine who, like Viola, uses her intelligence to survive misfortune. When her usurping uncle banishes her, she seeks refuge in the Forest of Arden, as had her father, the rightful Duke Senior. With her cousin and faithful friend, Celia, accompanying her, Rosalind adopts a male disguise originally to protect the two women from danger as they travel. Once in Arden, Celia reports that she has seen Orlando in the forest. Rosalind's first reaction is panic: "Alas the day, what shall I do with my doublet and hose?" (III, ii, 215).

When he appears, engaged in a witty interchange with the melancholy Jaques, she thinks quickly: "I will speak to him like a saucy lackey," she tells Celia (290). Her opening gambit is a conventional one—she asks him the time, to be told "there's no clock in the forest." She begins to improvise: "Time travels in divers paces with divers persons. I'll tell you who Time ambles withal, who Time trots withal, who Time gallops withal, and who he stands still withal" (302–305). After expounding on this topic with a display of her wit, she moves to the question of love and her uncle who taught her how to cure the lovesick. Knowing that the man she refers to is Orlando, she announces, "There is a man haunts the forest that abuses our young plants with carving 'Rosalind' on their barks. . . . If I could meet that fancy-monger, I would give him some good counsel, for he seems to have the quotidian[i] of love upon him" (350-56). Orlando admits it is he but insists "I would not be cured, youth." Rosalind persists, suggesting they meet every day and he woo her as if she were Rosalind, while she acts as Rosalind would—"changeable,

[i] fever

longing and liking, proud, fantastical, apish, shallow, inconstant, full of tears, full of smiles." He agrees.

The love game will be a release for them both; she can test Orlando's love without committing herself, and he can openly express his love to the "youth" enacting Rosalind as he never could face to face. (When she spoke to him at their first meeting, he could not utter a word, resorting to verse to declare his love.) Orlando's poems depict Rosalind as a nonpareil, while her diatribes, as Ganymede, go to the other extreme. The truth, Rosalind hopes he will learn, is somewhere in between. Realizing that she could not live up to the perfection Orlando endows her with, Rosalind must deflate the image. In their wooing game she reminds Orlando, almost with a touch of sadness, of the disappearance of illusion when "the sky changes" from courtship to the reality of marriage.[6] Then, humorously, she concocts a Rosalind it would be difficult to love:

> *Maids are May when they are maids, but the sky changes when they are wives. I will be more jealous of thee than a Barbary cock-pigeon over his hen, more clamorous than a parrot against rain. . . . I will weep for nothing. . . and I will do that when you are disposed to be merry. I will laugh like a hyen, and that when thou art inclined to sleep.*
> Orlando: *But will my Rosalind do so?*
> Rosalind: *By my life, she will do as I do.* (IV, i, 140–50)

The harder the test, the more Orlando meets its challenge. But he still must divest himself of his exaggerated language. When he says that he will die if Rosalind will not have him, Rosalind disparages his hyperbole in her effort to look for real love beneath the phraseology: "The poor world is almost six thousand years old, and in all this time there was not any man died in a love cause." Her witty examples of how Troilus and Leander really died have no effect on Orlando's exaggeration, as he replies, "I would not have my right Rosalind of this mind, for I protest her frown might kill me." "By this hand, it will not kill a fly," she responds (IV, i, 89–106). Orlando's reference to his "right Rosalind" is one of Shakespeare's reminders that Orlando, believing Ganymede is enacting Rosalind, plays this game only "because I would be talking of her" (85).

To give serious substance to the surface comedy, the audience is likewise constantly reminded of Rosalind, the woman under the Ganymede disguise. When Orlando promises to return in two hours, Rosalind cleverly conceals her anxiety to see him again, warning him that if he is a minute late, "I will think you the most pathetical break-promise, and the most hollow lover, and the most unworthy of her you call Rosalind, that may be chosen out of the gross band of the unfaithful: therefore beware my censure, and keep your promise." Still worshipful, Orlando replies, "With no less religion than if thou wert indeed my Rosalind: so adieu" (IV, i, 181–88). But as soon as he leaves, it is apparent that her disparagement is only by way of testing Orlando. She confesses to Celia "how many fathom deep I am in love. . . . I cannot be out of the sight of Orlando. I'll go find a shadow, and sigh till he come." Celia counters Rosalind's rhetorical attack on Cupid with a down-to-earth decision: "And I'll sleep" (195–208).

A lively and determined person on her own, Celia is also vital to the characterization of Rosalind. She is the listener to whom Rosalind can express her intentions or confess her true love for Orlando after she has been ridiculing him. It is Celia who softens Rosalind's satirical attacks on love and warns her against overdoing them. In sparkling commentary of her own, Celia can tease and provoke and bring Rosalind back to earth when she is in danger of being carried away by her flights of fancy. And she is always there to support Rosalind, to give her strength in the unknown territory into which she has ventured, in clothing of the opposite sex. She brings out the best in Rosalind, encouraging her bravery, responding sensibly to Rosalind's more outrageous sallies, and acting as a sounding board so that Rosalind may keep in touch with herself. Janet Suzman, who enacted Celia with the Royal Shakespeare Company, notes that "Celia, Touchstone, and the audience are the only ones who know the secret of Rosalind's disguise. The two central scenes of the play would be contrived and unacceptable, without Celia there to share the joke. . . . the danger of Celia giving the game away heightens the comedy."[7]

Shakespeare always knows exactly how long to sustain a situation and when to end it, a skill lesser playwrights might take note of. In the novel, Rosalind's clever remarks at the expense of her lover seem endless and eventually tiresome, but a novel may be put down and resumed again. In the play, the love banter ceases and shifts to a serious vein when Oliver enters with his brother Orlando's blood-soaked handkerchief. Rosalind's disguise is defeated when she responds emotionally to this sign of danger or death for Orlando—she faints. Orlando, hearing that Oliver and Celia are seriously in love, abandons the game, along with his overblown declarations of love. He tells Rosalind/Ganymede quite simply: "I can live no longer by thinking" (V, ii, 50). He has passed the test.

By taking charge of a situation that might defeat the less resourceful, Rosalind, banished from home and hopelessly in love, has found refuge, tested Orlando, and discovered him to be true. As she has determined the action, so she will resolve it. Using knowledge of magic taught her by an uncle seemingly invented on the spot, she will bring all together in the final sequence: "Jack shall have Jill / Nought shall go ill," as Puck predicts in *A Midsummer Night's Dream* (III, ii, 461–62). With Rosalind as giver and given, everyone receives a prize: The banished Duke Senior will be reunited with daughter Rosalind and with his dukedom, and four couples will be joined by Hymen, the god of marriage, who appears and pronounces: "Then is there mirth in heaven / When earthly things made even / Atone[i] together." Helen Gardner notes that "the great symbol of pure comedy is marriage by which the world is renewed, and its endings are always instinct with a sense of fresh beginnings."[8]

The serious theme of time and mutability, introduced lightly in Rosalind's first witty sally as Ganymede, is answered at the close by the song celebrating marriage and procreation, and the dance symbolizes, as it has done for centuries, the mutuality of marriage: "O blessed bond of board and bed: / 'Tis Hymen peoples every town (V, iv, 107-109, 141–42).

### *Much Ado About Nothing*—Beatrice

In *Much Ado About Nothing*, Beatrice is a woman who wittily disparages love to conceal her intense interest in it and in the object of her affections, Benedick. As she jests about love and marriage, insisting that she prefers to remain single, her style is

[i] accord

a unique combination of the down-to-earth and personal with the musical and universal. She replies to Don Pedro's comment that "Out o' question, you were born in a merry hour": "No sure my lord, my mother cried; but then there was a star danced, and under that was I born" (II, i, 313–16).

Recognizing both the pain and the joy of birth, she combines the everyday and the cosmic in a sentence of monosyllables except for the two-syllable balanced internal slant/rhyming "mother" and "under." After the harshness of the r's and the choppy pace of the first half, the music of the second line starts to sing with n's, beginning with "then," and lifts with assonance in "danced," "star," and "was."

As the play opens, a messenger brings news of Benedick's arrival, prompting denigrating remarks by Beatrice. Her uncle Leonato explains, "There is a kind of merry war betwixt Signior Benedick and her: they never meet but there's a skirmish of wit between them" (I, i, 55–58). War was a favorite metaphor for love, appearing in the sonnets of Dante and Petrarch as well as in those of the Elizabethans, including Shakespeare. Barbara Everett sees the play as a "dance-battle of two worlds," a clash of men's and women's worlds with Beatrice and Benedick as leading figures.[9] In the 1993 film, Emma Thompson as Beatrice and Kenneth Branagh as Benedick delivered their dialogue with deftness, allowing some serious depth as well, so that not all was froth. In his direction, Mr. Branagh maintained throughout a spirit of festivity that was rooted in reality.

Beatrice is not only critical of Benedick but mockingly self-deprecating as well. She responds to news of the match between Benedick's friend Claudio and her cousin Hero: "Good Lord for alliance: thus goes every one to the world but I, and I am sunburnt[i]; I may sit in a corner and cry 'Heigh-ho for a husband'" (II, i, 299–301). When Don Pedro asks if she would consider him as a husband, she responds with a metaphor based on clothing: "No my lord, unless I might have another for working-days, your Grace is too costly to wear every day" (308–309). For someone who claims she will never marry, Beatrice's constant theme is marriage, all the while insisting she would be happy to die a spinster. At the beginning of act two,

[i] that is, unattractive; a fair complexion was considered more desirable

when the assembled company are discussing Count John, it is Beatrice who introduces Benedick's name, comparing him and John, and then declaring, "Lord, I could not endure a husband with a beard on his face. I had rather lie in the woolen"[i] (linking the mention of a husband with an allusion to the marriage bed).

Leonato: *You may light on a husband that hath no beard.*
Beatrice: *What should I do with him? Dress him in my apparel and make him my waiting-gentlewoman? He that hath a beard is more than a youth, and he that hath no beard is less than a man; and he that is more than a youth is not for me; and he that is less than a man I am not for him.* (II, i, 26–35)

She wittily resigns herself to the fate of women who do not marry, that is, she will "lead apes in hell," but she puts a new twist on the old saying:

Leonato: *Well then, go you into hell?*
Beatrice: *No, but to the gate, and there will the Devil meet me . . . and say, "Get you to heaven, Beatrice, get you to heaven, here's no place for you maids." So deliver I up my apes, and away to Saint Peter, for the heavens; he shows me where the bachelors sit, and there live we as merry as the day is long.* (II, i, 35–45)

Although Beatrice puts a clever spin on what might be realities that are too harsh to accept otherwise, she is quick to criticize what she sees as injustice, like patriarchal choice of a marriage partner. When Claudio asks not Hero but her father for her hand in marriage, her uncle remarks, "Well, niece, I trust you will be ruled by your father." Before Hero can reply, Beatrice sharpens her wit on the custom: "Yes, faith, it is my cousin's duty to make curtsy and say, 'Father as it please you.' But yet for all that, cousin, let him be a handsome fellow, or else make another curtsy and say, 'Father, as it please me'" (II, i, 46–52).

By a ruse that her friends practice on her, Beatrice changes abruptly when she is made to believe that Benedick is desperately and hopelessly in love with her; his friends will use a similar trick to convince Benedick of Beatrice's love. Neither will need much convincing, as the disparagement of the other on both their parts, as well as their mutual insistence on

[i] a rough blanket

independence, was only a cover for their love. Their fear of rejection removed, each will rush to embrace a new-found commitment.

At the beginning of act three, in a scene entirely in verse, the women, under cover, set their plot in motion. Hearing that she is being discussed, Beatrice approaches the "false sweet bait" Ursula and Hero are setting out:

> Ursula: *But are you sure*
> *That Benedick loves Beatrice so entirely?*
> Hero: *So says the Prince and my new-troth'ed lord.* (III, i, 36–38)

Hero says she has persuaded them to "wish him wrestle with affection / And never to let Beatrice know of it," because Beatrice will never accept him:

> *Nature never framed a woman's heart*
> *Of prouder stuff than that of Beatrice.*
> *Disdain and scorn ride sparkling in her eyes,*
> *Misprising what they look on, and her wit*
> *Values itself so highly, that to her*
> *All matter else seems weak: she cannot love,*
> *Nor take no shape nor project of affection,*
> *She is so self-endeared.* (III, i, 49–56)

Although Hero exaggerates, as she does in detailing Benedick's virtues, there is truth in the description, and Beatrice realizes it:

> *What fire is in mine ears? Can this be true?*
> *Stand I condemned for pride and scorn so much?*
> *Contempt, farewell, and maiden pride, adieu.*
> *No glory lives behind the back of such.*
> *And Benedick, love on, I will requite thee.* (III, i, 107–11)

Her style has changed as well at her attitude, described in a ten-line sonnet, the traditional Elizabethan form for expressing love, as in the meeting of Romeo and Juliet.

In the quiet interlude just before the emotional denunciation of Hero in the church, the four women gather that morning in her chamber. It is one of Shakespeare's "women's world" indoor scenes where women converse about subjects they would hesitate to discuss in public. After first examining her wedding gown and its fashion, they move to a discussion of the wedding night, and the conversation takes a bawdy turn. A changed Beatrice appears, moping about love and complaining of a cold, which Margaret ventures might be cured by essence of "carduus benedictus" (a medicine) laid to her heart. As if Shakespeare were reluctant to abandon the witty remarks of Beatrice, he now assigns them to Margaret. Beatrice asks her, "How long have you professed apprehension?" that is, a quick wit, to which Margaret replies, "Ever since you left it" (III, iv, 63–64).

As the plot darkens with the episode at the altar, where Claudio rejects Hero, both Beatrice and Benedick, sobered by this event, discard their earlier banter and speak simply and from the heart:

> Benedick: *I do love nothing in the world as well as you—is not that strange?*
> Beatrice: *As strange as the thing I know not. It were as possible for me to say I loved nothing so well as you, but believe me not; and yet I lie not.* (IV, i, 266–70)

Almost like Portia declaring and then withdrawing her love in *The Merchant of Venice,* Beatrice seems reluctant at first, advancing and retreating. Emboldened by their friends' ruse to bring them together, now each uses simple language to state true feelings.

> Beatrice: *You have stayed me in a happy hour, I was about to protest I loved you.*
> Benedick: *And do it with all thy heart.*
> Beatrice: *I love you with so much of my heart that none is left to protest.*
> Benedick: *Come, bid me do anything for thee.*
> Beatrice: *Kill Claudio.*
> Benedick: *Ha, not for the wide world.*
> Beatrice: *You kill me to deny it. Farewell. . . .*
> Benedick: *Tarry, good Beatrice. By this hand I love thee.*
> Beatrice: *Use it for my love some other way than swearing by it.*
> Benedick: *Think you in your soul the Count Claudio hath wronged Hero?*
> Beatrice: *Yea, as sure as I have a thought, or a soul.*
> Benedick: *Enough, I am engaged, I will challenge him.*
> (IV, i, 282-330)

Once again, male friendship becomes secondary to commitment to a woman, and with predictably direr consequences than in *The Merchant of Venice*. *Much Ado* being a comedy, Benedick will not be required to kill his friend, but the fact that he is willing to do so for Beatrice reveals his new maturity as well as his deep love. As the good partner he gives promise of becoming, he is sensitive to Beatrice's feelings and gives her wishes precedence over his friendship with Claudio.

With the resolution of the mock death of Hero, Claudio's penance, and her restoration, Beatrice and Benedick resume their old bantering for the benefit of the assembled company. But when their friends produce love sonnets by each, they grudgingly admit their loves with the sparkle that characterizes the pair who begot the high style of Restoration comedy:

> Benedick: *Here's our own hands against our hearts. Come, I will have thee, but by this light, I take thee for pity.*
> Beatrice: *I would not deny you, but by this good day, I yield upon great persuasion, and partly to save your life, for I was told you were in a consumption.* (V, iv, 91–96)

At the end, the garden dance of the entire cast in the Branagh-Thompson film, winding in and out of Italianate shrubbery, demonstrates the spirit of joy that characterizes the endings of Shakespeare's comedies.

## Notes

[1] Alice Griffin, *The Sources of Ten Shakespearean Plays*, 209–26.

[2] C. L. Barber, *Shakespeare's Festive Comedy*, 247.

[3] J. M. Lothian and T. W. Craik, eds., *Twelfth Night*, Arden ed., 145 n.

[4] Barber, *Shakespeare's Festive Comedy*, 244.

[5] Thomas Lodge, *Rosalynde*, in *Elizabethan Prose Fiction*, ed. Merritt Lawlis, 278–294.

[6] Barber, *Shakespeare's Festive Comedy*, 236.

[7] Janet Suzman, *"As You Like It,"* in *Shakespeare: The Comedies*, ed. Robert Sales, 56.

[8] Helen Gardner, *"As You Like It,"* in *Shakespeare: The Comedies*, ed. Kenneth Muir, 61.

[9] Barbara Everett, *"Much Ado about Nothing,"* in *Critical Quarterly*, 3.4 (Winter 1961), 319.

# CHAPTER THREE: LATE COMEDIES

*The Winter's Tale* and *The Tempest*

The late comedies *The Winter's Tale* and *The Tempest*, written about 1610, share the themes of reconciliation, redemption, and rebirth. In both plays the love and courtship of the young pair stand in contrast to machinations by the older characters like the jealousy-crazed Leontes and the vengeful Prospero, both of whom experience transformation through forgiveness. Perdita and Miranda, and the men they marry at the end of the plays, symbolize the joy of love and hope for the future. Although they are appealing young women, they lack the diversity of the earlier heroines.

*The Winter's Tale*—Perdita

In the first half of *The Winter's Tale* Perdita is symbolic as the lost child, the abandoned baby whom the Oracle predicts must be found; otherwise her father, King Leontes, will die without an heir. After the troubles of her mother, Hermione, in prison and on trial, climaxed by her supposed death, the scene changes from the winter darkness at court to the summer brightness of a country festival. At age sixteen Perdita enters with her beloved, Prince Florizel. Both are in costume. He is a prince disguised as a rustic or country swain, in which guise he has been meeting her since a chance encounter when they fell in love at first sight. Perdita is named "Mistress of the Feast" by her foster-father, the shepherd who found and raised her, and she is "pranked up,"[i] as the goddess Flora. In her most famous passage she describes flowers that characterize the ages and symbolize rebirth.

[i] costumed

While Florizel's language of love is elaborate and filled with classical allusions, Perdita's is free of decoration; it is forthright and direct as she fears discovery:

*even now I tremble*
*To think your father, by some accident,*
*Should pass this way as you did.* (IV, iv, 18–20)

On that cue, in keeping with Shakespearean coincidence, King Polixenes and his courtier, Camillo, arrive in disguise at the sheep-shearing festival. Perdita greets them with flowers appropriate to their age, rosemary and rue, which "last all winter long." Her single lyric passage, describing and matching flowers of the seasons to the guests, is more than just a descriptive catalog, however beautiful and evocative. A serious note is introduced in her exchange with Polixenes about the cross-breeding of flowers, of which she disapproves. When Polixenes defends it as "an art which doth mend nature," she strikes a sad note of wishes unfulfilled:

*No more than were I painted*[i] *I would wish*
*This youth would say 'twere well and only therefore*
*Desire to breed by me.* (IV, iv, 101–103)

Soon Polixenes will be vehemently using her argument, not his, against the very union she refers to. Resuming her lyrical catalog of blooms, she gives to the middle-aged persons there "flowers of middle summer," suffused with the smells of midsummer:

*Hot lavender, mints, savory, marjoram,*
*The marigold that goes to bed wi' th' sun*
*And with him rises, weeping.* (IV, iv, 104–106)

After the serious note of the marigold, "weeping" with morning dew, she wishes she had "some flowers o' th' spring" for the young people present, and again sees the flowers as reflecting human destiny, perhaps her own, in the "pale primroses / That die unmarried." She concludes the passage by addressing Florizel, whose name, like hers as Flora, symbolizes flowers:

[i] streaked, like the cross-bred gilly flower she refuses to cultivate

*daffodils,*
*That come before the swallow dares, and take*
*The winds of March with beauty. Violets, dim,*
*But sweeter than the lids of Juno's eyes*
*Or Cytherea's breath; pale primroses*
*That die unmarried ere they can behold*
*Bright Phoebus in his strength (a malady*
*Most incident to maids); bold oxlips and*
*The crown imperial; lilies of all kinds,*
*The flower de luce being one. O these I lack*
*To make you garlands of; and my sweet friend,*
*To strew him o'er and o'er.* (IV, iv, 118–29)

Assonance creates the musical effect, sustained by the repetition of 'l' in each line, including the penultimate three lines when l's almost tumble over one another in a melody that ends with the repetition of two long, low diphthongs repeating the intermittent note of sadness.

Although Polixenes and Camillo praise Perdita during the "dance of Shepherds and Shepherdesses," her misgivings come true. As she and Florizel plight their troth, Polixenes, throwing off his disguise, interrupts the ceremony. Florizel chooses love over rank, defies his father, and decides to flee with Perdita from Bohemia. Camillo suggests his native Sicilia, and the couple return to the land of Perdita's birth. After they face another threatening situation, all is made known, the Oracle's prediction comes true, and the play ends with the magical scene of Hermione's return to life. Paulina stage-manages the scene:

*Turn, good lady,*
*Our Perdita is found.*
Hermione: *You gods, look down,*
*And from your sacred vials pour your graces*
*Upon my daughter's head. Tell me, mine own,*
*Where hast thou been preserved? Where lived?*
*How found thy father's court?* (V, iii, 120–25)

Although she kneels for her mother's blessing, Perdita is given no opportunity to reply, as Paulina interjects: "There's time enough for that," nor does Perdita speak again before the play ends. Yet her presence is important, symbolizing the future and the family Leontes thought he had lost. The plot of this romance is so crowded with incident in which the characters of Leontes, Hermione, and Paulina are developed that Perdita remains an appealing symbol of rebirth, like the flowers she describes in her one major scene in act four.

*The Tempest*—Miranda

Miranda in *The Tempest* in some way resembles Perdita. Both undergo hardships as babies, both are brought up in adversity and Cinderella-like end by marrying a prince. But Miranda, in this last comedy and last solo work by Shakespeare, is a more memorable character. Her name, like Perdita's, describes her. Miranda means "admire," which to Elizabethans meant "to wonder at." From the first scene of the shipwreck that she beholds, Miranda conveys to the audience—and in a sense shares with them—her wonderment at the magical effect of the events that ensue.

Brought to the island at the age of two by her banished father, Prospero, she has been raised and tutored by him. Prospero's white magic is countered by the magic of love in the first meeting between Miranda and Ferdinand when they fall in love at first sight. In her naiveté, Miranda, who has seen no men other than her father and Caliban, wonders whether Ferdinand might be one of the spirits Prospero commands:

*What is't? A spirit?*
*Lord, how it looks about. Believe me sir,*
*It carries a brave*[i] *form. But 'tis a spirit.* (I, ii, 412–14)

When Prospero assures her she is seeing another human being, she insists,

*I might call him*
*A thing divine, for nothing natural*
*I ever saw so noble.* (I, ii, 420–22)

Her dialogue is simple, yet eloquent in its simplicity, as if Shakespeare in this last play had honed away all the rhetorical devices, leaving the essential beauty of the lines, beauty coupled with wonder. When Ferdinand asks Miranda her name and she tells him, he replies, "Admired Miranda, / Indeed the top of admiration[ii]" (III, i, 37–38). Her name is a key to her dialogue as

[i] handsome [ii] wonder

well as to her character. Filled with wonder, she describes the assemblage at the end as a "brave new world" that has arrived at the island. Never one to present only a single point of view, Shakespeare includes among the "goodly creatures" at whom she wonders not only Ferdinand and Gonzalo but also usurpers, drunkards, thieves, and would-be murderers.

In their second scene together, Ferdinand is carrying logs, a task set him by Prospero, who has both willed the match and imposed hardships on Ferdinand:

*They are both in either's powers: but this swift business*
*I must uneasy make, lest too light*[i] *winning*
*Make the prize light.*[ii] (I, ii, 453–55)

Ferdinand is piling the logs when Miranda addresses him in terms that are simple and straightforward, yet imaginative in the metaphor based on close observation: the weeping log. Again, like the weeping marigold in *The Winter's Tale* (IV, iv, 110), Shakespeare introduces a sad note into dialogue of love:

*Work not so hard; I would the lightning had*
*Burnt up those logs that you are enjoined to pile.*
*Pray set it down and rest you: when this burns*
*'Twill weep*[iii] *for having wearied you.* (III, i, 16–19)

Miranda may be naive and wondering, but she is no weakling. She offers practical reasons why she should carry the logs in his place:

*It will become me*
*As well as it does you, and I should do it*
*With much more ease, for my good will is to it,*
*And yours it is against.* (III, i, 28–31)

Using hyperbole that Miranda is unaccustomed to hearing, he declares himself her slave, to which Miranda responds with a direct question: "Do you love me?" (67). Again Ferdinand asserts his love, and Miranda, like all her predecessors in the plays, is the first to suggest marriage:

*Hence, bashful cunning*
*And prompt me, plain and holy innocence:*
*I am your wife if you will marry me,*

[i] easy [ii] unvalved [iii] that is, resin, which the burning log exudes

*If not, I'll die your maid.* (III, i, 81–84)

When Ferdinand's reply is enigmatic: "My mistress dearest, And I thus humble ever," Miranda persists, "My husband then?" (III, i, 86–87).

Prospero later warns the young man that he must not "break her virgin-knot before / All sanctimonious ceremonies may, / With full and holy rite, be ministered" (IV, i, 15–17). With a straightforward description of the marriage he anticipates, Ferdinand vows to respect Miranda's body, "As I hope / For quiet days, fair issue,[i] and long life" (23–24).

In honor of the union, Prospero will direct his spirits to present a show like those in *A Midsummer Night's Dream* and *Love's Labour's Lost*, which may have celebrated a royal marriage or visit when the play was seen at court. Here Juno, the goddess of marriage, and Ceres, the goddess of plenty, join to "bless this twain, that they may prosperous be, / And honored in their issue." Juno wishes them "Long continuance, and increasing," and Ceres "Earth's increase, foison plenty" (IV, i, 105–10).

As the show vanishes, the goddesses' joyful themes of marriage and procreation turn somber with Proteus's reminder of the mutability that marriage addresses:

*And like the baseless fabric of this vision,*
*The cloud-capped towers, the gorgeous palaces,*
*The solemn temples, the great globe itself,*
*Yea, all which it inherit, shall dissolve,*
*And like this insubstantial pageant faded,*
*Leave not a rack[ii] behind.* (IV, i, 151–56)

In the final scene Ferdinand and Miranda are introduced in a stylized stage picture. Prospero draws the curtain of the inner stage and discloses a tableau: "Ferdinand and Miranda playing at chess." Possibly because of the intricate moves of its carved pieces representing people, the game of chess was depicted as a symbol of courtship and marriage in medieval woodcuts and literature as well as on wedding chests. Chaucer's Criseyde, an independent woman, is reluctant to remarry: "Shall noon housbonde seyn to me 'chek mat!'"( I, 751). And T. S. Eliot includes two wearisome marriages in the section "A Game of

[i] children

[ii] cloud, also the technical name for clouds in court shows or masques

Chess" in *The Waste Land,* a poem in which allusions to *The Tempest* represent past glory contrasted with present desolation.

Ferdinand kneels for the blessing of his father, the King of Naples, and Miranda marvels at the "brave new world / That has such people in't," evoking Prospero's comment, born of experience, "'Tis new to thee" (V, i, 183–84). Prospero forgoes revenge and forgives his former enemies. Gonzalo rejoices in the happy and positive ending:

> *Ferdinand . . . found a wife,*
> *Where he himself was lost: Prospero, his dukedom*
> *In a poor isle: and all of us, ourselves,*
> *When no man was his own.* (V, i, 210–13)

# CHAPTER FOUR: TRAGEDIES

*Romeo and Juliet* and *Hamlet*

*Romeo and Juliet*—Juliet

The tragedy *Romeo and Juliet* ends not with a dance symbolizing marriage, as do many of the comedies, but with death. That Romeo and Juliet are "star-crossed" and "death-marked" is made known in the prologue, yet their struggle to attain love and their passionate commitment to each other have made the pair irresistibly sympathetic to audiences for over 400 years, since the play was first performed "with great applause." It is so advertised on the 1597 Quarto title page, which omits Shakespeare's name. From the moment they meet at the Capulet feast the couple create their own world, bounded by their love and isolated from a hostile society and the hatred of the blood feud that will destroy them. It is a world where cosmic imagery describes the wonder and joy of love that is both physical and spiritual, expressed in their first meeting and building in intensity as the action progresses through the balcony scene, the marriage, the parting, and the final irony of mistimed deaths in the tomb.

Under the influence of love, both grow to a rich maturity, Juliet's perhaps the more impressive, as she is literally an obedient child in her first scene. At the age of thirteen, she is summoned by her mother, Lady Capulet, who announces that Lord Capulet has spoken with Count Paris about marriage to Juliet. This was no surprise to the original audience, as the age of consent then was thirteen, and Lady Capulet reports that she was already a mother at Juliet's age. Juliet has five lines in a scene of one hundred and five. When her mother asks, "How stands your dispositions to be married?" she replies, "It is an honor that I dream not of" (I, iii, 65–66). The nurse recounts an incident from Juliet's babyhood, with a bawdy punchline, and Lady Capulet enumerates at length the merits of suitor Paris, concluding, "Can you like of Paris' love?" Juliet's three-line rhymed response is her longest speech in the scene:

*I'll look to like, if looking liking move,*
*But no more deep will I endart mine eye*
*Than your consent gives strength to make it fly.* (I, iii, 97–99)

It has been noted that the play is built on contrasts—love with hate, light with dark, night with day, age with youth, crowds with isolation, life with death, and Mercutio's and the nurse's equation of love as sex with Romeo's and Juliet's all-encompassing love. The two lovers also are contrasted, as their opening scenes demonstrate. Romeo, being male and somewhat older, is free to go about the streets of Verona with his friends Mercutio and Benvolio, looking for and participating in street fighting prompted by the feud. Believing he is in love with Rosaline, who rejects his love, he behaves like a typical courtly lover—sleepless, moody, and withdrawn from society. Juliet is at home, where young women at the time were expected to be, accepting direction from her parents. As the play begins, both are recognizable types. Under the influence of love, all this changes.

That Romeo is truly in love at first sight with Juliet is clear from the change in his style. Gone is the artificiality of his earlier declarations about Rosaline, as he exclaims upon seeing Juliet: "O she doth teach the torches to burn bright" (I, v, 43). Their first exchange of words is in the form of a sonnet, traditionally used to express love. The overall metaphor is that of a pilgrim approaching the shrine of a saint, the religious overtones supplying depth and sincerity to the simplicity of the language. Now Juliet, inspired by love, replies in a sophisticated way, by extending the metaphor and gently reprimanding him for asking to kiss her hand: "For saints have hands that pilgrims' hands do touch, / And palm to palm is holy palmers' kiss" (I, v, 98–99). When Romeo persists and asks to kiss her lips—"Have not saints lips and holy palmers too?"—she wittily counters his request: "Ay, pilgrim, lips that they must use in prayer." In her next line, she is suggesting that she might "grant" him a kiss, and when he does kiss her, she responds by obliquely asking for another: "Then have my lips the sin that they have took." His second kiss prompts her comment "You kiss by the book" (as if he had learned kissing from a book), which suggests that kissing is a new experience for both (99–109). By the end of the evening, Juliet has grown from an obedient child to a young woman who can handle her side of a love exchange and who can deviously ask her nurse about Romeo's identity.

In the balcony scene, Romeo continues to speak like a sonneteer, although the intensity of his lines testifies to their sincerity. She is the more direct and the more practical from the beginning. When she worries about the danger to him from her kinsmen, Romeo resorts to hyperbole:

> Juliet: *If they do see thee, they will murder thee.*
> Romeo: *Alack, there lies more peril in thine eye*
> *Than twenty of their swords.* (II, ii, 70–72)

Her simple question—"By whose direction found'st thou out this place?"—receives a reply based on the god of love, Cupid, who is traditionally pictured as blind: "By love, that did prompt me to enquire. / He lent me counsel, and I lent him eyes." In the longest passage in the scene, Juliet again speaks with directness, using few figures of speech, simply an explanation that she cannot be coy or flirtatious as he already has overheard her confess her love for him. She asks the same of him: "If thou dost love, pronounce it faithfully" (94). Yet she is careful to protect her image lest he think her too forward:

> *If thou think'st I am too quickly won,*
> *I'll frown and be perverse and say thee nay,*
> *So thou wilt woo; but else, not for the world.* (II, ii, 95–97)

Her twenty-one-line speech ends with a rhetorical flourish, asking that he "not impute this yielding to light love / Which the dark night hath so discover'ed." It is Juliet who injects a note of caution into the ecstatic lyricism of the scene:

> *Although I joy in thee,*
> *I have no joy of this contract tonight:*
> *It is too rash, too unadvised, too sudden,*
> *Too like the lightning, which doth cease to be*
> *Ere one can say 'It lightens.'* (II, ii, 116–20)

And it is Juliet who takes the initiative and asks directly about specific arrangements for marriage:

*If that thy bent of love be honorable,*
*Thy purpose marriage, send me word tomorrow*
*By one that I'll procure to come to thee,*
*Where and what time thou wilt perform the rite*
*And all my fortunes at thy foot I'll lay*
*And follow thee my lord throughout the world.* (II, ii, 143–48)

Her imagery in this scene is based on the everyday; its expression makes the ordinary extraordinary. "The mask of night" as a delicate reference to their first meeting when Romeo was masked; the lightning; their "bud of love"; and the little bird, to which she likens her desire to keep Romeo with her—and possibly under her control—although she knows the coming light of dawn will be dangerous for him:

*I would have thee gone,*
*And yet no farther than a wanton's*[i] *bird,*
*That lets it hop a little from his hand*
*Like a poor prisoner in his twisted gyves*[ii]
*And with a silken thread plucks it back again,*
*So loving-jealous of his liberty.* (II, ii, 176–81)

Her two classical references, to Jove (93) and Echo (161), are conventional, yet suggest learning, which was on the increase for young girls of Shakespeare's day.

Juliet has two long soliloquies, which contrast with each other. In the first, imagery and emotion combine in an epithalamium, or song celebrating a marriage, as she awaits their wedding night. No longer is she speaking of the everyday, like buds and birds; the very rush of the lines and the allusions suggest how much she has matured. The unusual, far-fetched imagery or "conceits" indicate imagination as well as the deep love that inspires them. The entire soliloquy centers on Romeo. Anxious for night and Romeo to arrive, she prophetically alludes to Phaëthon, son of Apollo, the sun god, who disobeyed his father and stole his chariot but died when he could not restrain its horses from galloping wildly away. She eagerly longs for night to bring consummation of their marriage, their "amorous

[i] youngster's [ii] manacles

rites," which she combines with their need for secrecy in the dark of "love-performing" night, which curtains them as did the conventional hangings around beds:

*Spread thy close curtain, love-performing night,*
*That runaways' eyes may wink,*[i] *and Romeo*
*Leap to these arms, untalked of and unseen.*
*Lovers can see to do their amorous rites*
*By their own beauties.* (III, ii, 5–9)

In a reversal of the common fear of the dark, night is friendly to the pair, and day is hostile; night joins them and day parts them.[1] Juliet invokes night and Romeo in a series of contrasts—darkness and brightness, winning and losing (her virginity), black and white, shining and garish—concluding with a "conceit" or extended figure, perhaps the most striking and imaginative in the play so far:

*Come gentle night, come loving, black-browed night,*
*Give me my Romeo, and when he shall die,*
*Take him and cut him out in little stars,*
*And he will make the face of heaven so fine,*
*That all the world will be in love with night,*
*And pay no worship to the garish sun.* (III, ii, 20–25)

This final image introduces the death motif, which has been sounding throughout in a minor key, but which will intensify as the action progresses.

With the entry of the nurse delivering news of Romeo's banishment, Juliet must find resources to survive a new and threatening situation. Although at first she joins the nurse in berating Romeo for killing Tybalt, she reasons that as Romeo's wife, she must defend him and that Tybalt might have killed him:

*Ah poor my lord, what tongue shall smooth thy name,*
*When I thy three-hours wife have mangled it?*
*But wherefore villain didst thou kill my cousin?*
*That villain cousin would have killed my husband:*
*Back foolish tears, back to your native spring.* (III, ii, 98–102)

In contrast, Romeo, in Friar Lawrence's cell, weeps, threatens to kill himself, and falls on the floor, until the friar consoles him

[i] close the eyes and keep them shut

and promises to intercede with the feuding families. The nurse, with a few unintentionally bawdy puns, assists by falsely reporting that Juliet is behaving likewise (III, iii).

"Three-hours wife" is a reminder of how swiftly events are moving. In the parting the morning after their wedding night, Juliet again alludes to birds, trying to hold back time by saying it is the nightingale they hear, not the lark, and that it is not daylight, but a meteor, to be a torchbearer—a reminder of Romeo's earlier entry to the Capulet party—to light Romeo on his way. Again, Romeo's lines are more lyrical and Juliet's more down to earth and immediate, including her chilling foreboding after he has climbed down from the upper-stage and she remains above: "Methinks I see thee, now thou art so low, / As one dead in the bottom of a tomb" (III, v, 55–56).

As Romeo departs to banishment, Lady Capulet enters to inform Juliet of her imminent marriage to Paris, which has been arranged by her father. In a contrast to her earlier scene of childlike obedience, Juliet's refusal astonishes her parents. Conversing with her mother, Juliet must demonstrate a newly acquired skill at equivocation by implying that she would like to get her hands on Romeo to wreak her revenge (a cover for her physical longing for him). Her father, solicitous of her feelings in his earlier talk with Paris (I, ii), now, to reinforce his hasty decision to arrange their wedding without even consulting Juliet, is angered at his daughter's refusal:

*And you be mine, I'll give you to my friend,*
*And you be not, hang, beg, starve, die in the streets,*
*For by my soul I'll ne'er acknowledge thee.* (III, v, 191–93)

Shocked at meeting Paris in Friar Lawrence's cell, Juliet must retain her composure and speak almost flirtatiously with him, when he asks:

*Come you to make confession to this father?*
Juliet: *To answer that, I should confess to you.*
Paris: *Do not deny to him that you love me.*
Juliet: *I will confess to you that I love him.* (IV, i , 22–25)

The greatest test so far of Juliet's determination and strength of character is her decision to avoid the marriage to Paris by taking the potion Friar Lawrence has given her, even though it may be fatal. In her second soliloquy (act four scene three), she considers all the dangers of taking the potion, asking herself questions and supplying the answers: What if the potion is poison? But the friar always has demonstrated that he is "a holy man." What if she wakes before Romeo arrives? Might she suffocate? Could the very surroundings drive her out of her mind, to pick up one of the bones and kill herself? She puts an end to these morbid thoughts by drinking off the potion as if it were a toast to Romeo: "Romeo I come: this do I drink to thee" (58).

The Liebestod, or love-death motif, reaches a crescendo on the morning of the day she is to marry Paris. Juliet is discovered under the influence of the potion, believed to be dead. Amidst the moaning and weeping, Capulet informs Paris:

> *O son, the night before thy wedding day*
> *Hath Death lain with thy wife: there she lies,*
> *Flower as she was, deflower'ed by him:*
> *Death is my son-in-law, Death is my heir,*
> *My daughter he hath wedded.* (IV, v, 35–39)

The love-death theme resounds through the final scene in the tomb. Romeo's final, long soliloquy of thirty-five lines is some of the best poetry in the play, as he builds on Capulet's earlier image of death as "amorous" of Juliet, whose "beauty makes / This vault a feasting presence full of light." His drinking the poison as a toast—"Here's to my love" (119)—echoes Juliet's taking the potion.

Juliet awakens just moments later, to hear from the friar of Romeo's death: "Thy husband in thy bosom there lies dead" (155). With a world of sad maturity, she refuses the friar's offer to depart with him, kisses Romeo in the hope that some poison may remain on his lips, and speaks what are possibly the most poignant words in all drama: "Thy lips are warm." She takes the dagger he is wearing and stabs herself in a final image in which her body is the receptacle of his: "This is thy sheath, there rust and let me die" (169).

Shakespeare's source is a long poem by Arthur Brooke, published in 1562, translated from the French version of an Italian story by Matteo Bandello. A moralist, Brooke prefaces his English version with a warning to readers that the tragic ending of Romeo and Juliet is punishment for disobedience to their parents. Brooke believes that a function of storytelling is to provide examples of such bad behavior: "the good man's example biddeth men to be good, and the evil man's mischief warneth men not to be evil."[2] Shakespeare, however, blames the parents. As the prince says at the end:

*Capulet, Montague,*
*See what a scourge is laid upon your hate,*
*That heaven finds means to kill your joys with love.* (V, iii, 291–93)

Scenes from the play in its latest film incarnation, *Shakespeare in Love,* co-authored by Tom Stoppard and expertly acted by Gwyneth Paltrow and Joseph Fiennes, are a commentary on Elizabethan stage practices as well as a relevant reminder of the work's universal and timeless appeal. In 1996 the Buz Luhrmann film version with Claire Danes and Leonardo DiCaprio in the leads earned popularity and new audiences by its innovative modern setting that preserved the original dialogue. The introductory chorus was delivered as a television news report, gang warfare was waged with guns brand-named "sword," and the balcony scene incorporated a swimming pool.

*Hamlet*—Ophelia

There can be no question that Hamlet is in love with Ophelia and she with him, as the text makes clear. Her father's and brother's warnings against Hamlet might send a more determined young woman right into his arms, after already receiving his letters, gifts, and messages. But Ophelia, complaisant under the demands of patriarchy, is as obedient as was Juliet in her first scene. Her father, Polonius, has been described as displaying "dotage encroaching upon wisdom," but he shows much dotage and very little wisdom in his treatment of his daughter. In Hamlet's epitaph for Polonius, he is aptly described as a "wretched, rash, intruding fool"(III, iv, 31). First, Polonius is wrong in advising Ophelia that "Lord Hamlet is a prince out of thy star, / This must not be" (II, ii, 140–41). He believes that Prince Hamlet is too high in rank to marry Ophelia; he is out of her "sphere." However, the queen says at Ophelia's grave,

*I hoped thou shouldst have been my Hamlet's wife:*
*I thought thy bride-bed to have decked, sweet maid,*
*And not have strewed thy grave.* (V, i, 237–39)

Not only does Polonius tell Ophelia that Hamlet will not marry her, but he makes her return his gifts, refuse his messages, and "lock herself from his resort" (II, ii, 143–44). Hamlet's love letter to Ophelia, which her father reads to the assembled court, addresses her as "my soul's idol" and states, "But that I love thee best, O most best, believe it" (109, 120–21). When he leaps into her grave, he declares,

*I loved Ophelia. Forty thousand brothers*
*Could not with all their quantity of love*
*Make up my sum.* (V, i, 264–66)

Being completely dominated by her father, told what to do and what to think, Ophelia is never allowed the opportunity to make her own decisions. In her scenes with her brother, her father, and Hamlet, she reacts to what they say. Rarely does she make a positive or assertive statement. She first appears with her brother, Laertes, who warns her about Hamlet—she is not to hope that he might choose her as his wife without consulting the state.

*Then if he says he loves you,*
*It fits your wisdom so far to believe it*
*As he in his particular act and place*
*May give his saying deed; which is no further*
*Than the main voice*[i] *of Denmark goes withal.* (I, iii, 24–28)

So she must not heed his declarations of love "or your chaste treasure open / To his unmastered importunity" (31-32). After she listens to Laertes's advice, her speech reveals she has some spirit, though repressed, when she suggests that he

*Do not as some ungracious pastors do,*
*Show me the steep and thorny way to heaven,*
*Whiles like a puffed and reckless libertine*
*Himself the primrose path of dalliance treads.* (I, iii, 47–50)

After Laertes departs for France, Polonius questions Ophelia about Hamlet. When she says that Hamlet has "made many tenders / Of his affection to me" (99–100), Polonius asks, "Do you believe his tenders, as you call them?" Ophelia's reply reveals how completely she is dominated by her father:

[i] vote

Ophelia: *I do not know my lord what I should think.*
Polonius: *Marry, I will teach you.* (I, iii, 104–105)

The scene ends with his instructing her not to "give words or talk with the Lord Hamlet," to which Ophelia replies, as she most likely always has, "I shall obey, my lord."

When Hamlet decides to "put an antic disposition on" (I, v, 180)—that is, to play mad while planning his revenge against King Claudius—he tries out his mad role on Ophelia, evidently aware that she will report it immediately to Polonius, as she does. Polonius is again wrong when he decides that Hamlet's madness is caused by love, and he hastens to the king and queen with the love letter Ophelia has dutifully given him:

*This in obedience hath my daughter shown me,*
*And more above, hath his solicitings,*
*As they fell out by time, by means, and place,*
*All given to mine ear.* (II, ii, 124–27)

When the king is not convinced by Polonius's theory that Hamlet's "madness" is due to rejected love, it is Polonius's idea to "loose my daughter to him," while he and the king hide behind an arras, or curtain, to watch the encounter. "Loose" is a particularly ugly word in this context, as it applies to the coupling of livestock.

Polonius stage-directs Ophelia for this encounter with Hamlet:

*Ophelia, walk you here. . . . Read on this book,*
*That show of such an exercise may color*[i]
*Your loneliness.* (III, i, 43–46)

Why is Hamlet so cruel—verbally—to Ophelia in this scene? Two reasons seem the most probable. Having learned from the ghost what he must do, Hamlet wishes to separate Ophelia, whom he loves, from the blood-bath he is about to enter—murdering the head of state is a dangerous business. Second, it is very likely that in this scene, as it is usually acted, he spots some movement behind the arras. Suspecting the king, Hamlet's method of convincing him of madness is to speak as no courtier would to the lady he loves. Practically every sentence is an obscenity, telling her to go to a nunnery[ii] and asking if she is "honest."[iii] David Leverenz points out that the mixed signals of

[i] excuse [ii] brothel (slang) [iii] chaste

Ophelia's acceptance and then rejection of Hamlet's love "since he has no knowledge of her obedience to Polonius' command, so evokes Gertrude's inconstancy that Hamlet's double messages to Ophelia take on a frenzied condemnation of all women."[3] He is insulting not only to her but to womankind in general, prompted by his disgust at his mother's adulterous relationship with Claudius. And now the woman he loves is rejecting him, as he believes his mother has done. Two clues suggest that Hamlet notices some movement behind the arras. First, he asks Ophelia where her father is; in her confusion she lies: "at home, my lord." Second, he issues a direct challenge to the hidden king: "We will have no mo marriage. Those that are married already—all but one—shall live" (III, i, 103, 121, 130, 149–50).

It is a demeaning scene for Ophelia to have been forced to play. It is obvious from her immediate lament that she does love Hamlet, and she is completely unsettled by his behavior and by the change in him from "the courtier's, soldier's, scholar's, eye, tongue, sword" to "quite, quite down." She ends by describing the effect on her:

*And I of ladies most deject and wretched*
*That sucked the honey of his music vows,*
*Now see that noble and most sovereign reason*
*Like sweet bells jangled out of tune and harsh. . . .*
*O woe is me*
*To have seen what I have seen, see what I see.* (III, i, 153–63)

Although Ophelia is distraught, the king and Polonius pay little attention to her as they emerge from behind the arras. Polonius merely tells her that she "need not tell us what Lord Hamlet said / We heard it all" (181–82). He is busy proposing to the king another session of spying on Hamlet.

At the play-within-the-play with the courtiers present, Hamlet speaks even more obscenely to Ophelia, and she is so embarrassed that she can reply to such affronts with only a few words.

Hamlet: *Lady, shall I lie in your lap?*
Ophelia: *No, my lord.*
Hamlet: *I mean my head upon your lap.*
Ophelia: *Ay, my lord.*
Hamlet: *Do you think I meant country matters?*[i]

[i] fornication

Ophelia: *I think nothing my lord.*
Hamlet: *That's a fair thought to lie between maids' legs.*
Ophelia: *What is, my lord?*
Hamlet: *Nothing.*[i] (III, ii, 110-19)

So dependent has Ophelia been made by Polonius that when faced with a situation she cannot handle, she becomes almost inarticulate. Even worse is to follow. After Hamlet kills Polonius, Ophelia is alone. Laertes is abroad; her father, who directed her life, has been killed by the man she loves. Unable to face reality, Ophelia retreats into madness. It is ironic that when she is deprived of the patriarchy on which she had been forced to depend, she loses both her mind and her life.

In the songs she sings in her madness she mixes love with the obscenities that Hamlet had flung at her: "How should I your true love know" and a Valentine's day ballad about a maid whose lover refuses to marry her once he has bedded her (IV, v, 23–66). Her death by drowning, as the queen describes it in act four, scene seven, reflects the destiny of Ophelia as it has been shaped by Polonius; she is as helpless against the stream as she was against her father, and she is pulled down "to muddy death."

In the 1996 movie of *Hamlet* made by Kenneth Branagh, who plays the title role, Kate Winslet is the most effective Ophelia yet seen on film. She conveys the confusion of the young and dependent Ophelia in the early scenes and is entirely convincing in the mad scene, often overdone by actresses less expert. As this is film, Branagh is able to emphasize the love between Hamlet and Ophelia by depicting love scenes as recollection over their dialogue.

## Notes

[1] Mark Van Doren, *Shakespeare: Five Great Tragedies*, 3.

[2] Griffin, *Sources*, 3.

[3] Leverenz, "The Woman in Hamlet," in *Representing Shakespeare*, ed. Murray M. Schwartz and Coppelia Kahn, 119.

[i] nothing=0=vagina

# SECTION II.

## MARRIAGE

When the subject is courtship, all but one of Shakespeare's comedies end with marriage. In plays that begin with marriage or treat an established one, women face new problems. These vary from curing a husband's infidelity to defending against charges of hers, from pursuing and winning over a reluctant husband to abandoning selfhood for his goals, from overcoming hostility to achieving mutual respect. Farces like *The Taming of the Shrew* and *The Comedy of Errors* present women who descend from the medieval fabliaux, which depicted a wife as a shrew or scold, nagging and criticizing her husband, yet clever enough to extricate herself from compromising situations. Shakespeare's marriage comedies inherit from the fabliaux infidelity as a favorite topic—whether it is the husband's, as in *The Comedy of Errors,* or false accusations of the wife's in *The Merry Wives of Windsor.* In addition to these comedies, a wife charged with infidelity becomes a subject for romances like *The Winter's Tale* and *Cymbeline,* as well as for tragedy in *Othello.* In all these plays the wife is motivated by her love for her husband. In *King Lear* the evil sisters' extramarital lust for Edmund brings about their defeat.

# CHAPTER FIVE: FARCES

*The Taming of the Shrew, The Comedy of Errors,* and *The Merry Wives of Windsor*

## *The Taming of the Shrew*—Katherina

Katherina in *The Taming of the Shrew* both resembles and differs from the other heroines of Shakespeare's comedies. Like them, she is intelligent, well bred, witty, and in love. Unlike them, she is a shrew, a woman who is bad-tempered, sharp-tongued, and violent, a stock character of medieval fabliaux and ballads. But Shakespeare provides motivation for Kate. The unfavored elder daughter of Baptista, Kate may well be putting on a shrewish disposition as protection to ward off those who might reject her or curb her independence. Her bad temper is also her means of attracting her father's attention when all of his care is lavished on Bianca, the favored daughter. Kate's quick wit and gift for language offer the opportunity of an outlet; when she feels constrained, she at least has freedom of speech:

> *My tongue will tell the anger of my heart,*
> *Or else my heart concealing it will break,*
> *And rather than it shall, I will be free*
> *Even to the uttermost, as I please, in words.* (IV, iii, 77–80)

Bianca has three suitors, who are told by Baptista that they must wait until Katherina is married before he awards Bianca's hand in marriage. He may be displaying patriarchal privilege, but it is a foregone conclusion that each daughter will make her own choice. Penelope Mortimer notes that Shakespeare "seems to be saying in this play at least that a sensible deal between equals is a lot more satisfactory than a short-lived honeymoon, however ecstatic. When it came to marrying off his own daughters, Shakespeare was an old man in his early forties who found himself in something like Baptista's predicament. Susanna, 'witty above her sex,' married the admirable Dr. Hall and lived happily ever after. Judith romantically married Thomas Quiney, a n'er-do-well four years her junior and came to grief. I'm sure Dr. Hall behaved impeccably at the wedding, but I wonder whether Shakespeare would have preferred a less austere son-in-law for his favorite daughter's bridegroom."[1]

When Petruchio arrives in Padua seeking a wealthy wife, Bianca's suitors offer to finance his courtship of Katherina. Although they warn Petruchio about Kate's bad temper, nothing will deter him from his suit, as he explains in a soliloquy:

*Say that she rail, why then I'll tell her plain*
*She sings as sweetly as a nightingale.*
*Say that she frown, I'll say she looks as clear*
*As morning roses newly washed with dew.* (II, i, 170–73)

He will play the part of an even-tempered suitor and woo her in terms that may be conventional but that she had never heard addressed to herself before. Stage director Margaret Webster pointed out as far back as 1942 that in the wooing scene the couple must fall in love with each other, to make the rest of the play meaningful, to show that Petruchio tests Kate because he loves her, and this leads to a happy and mutually caring partnership.[2] Kate may be an early working of Beatrice in *Much Ado*, but not even that lady can match Kate when it comes to insults. In their first meeting, Petruchio follows his plan and lets nothing faze him. He will trade insults and will give as good as he takes:

Kate: *I knew you at the first.*
*You were a movable.*
Petruchio: *Why what's a movable?*
Kate: *A joint-stool.*
Petruchio: *Thou has hit it. Come sit on me.*
Kate: *Asses are made to bear, and so are you.*
Petruchio: *Women are made to bear*[i] *and so are you.*
(II, i, 197–200)

[i] that is, children

Petruchio uses every opportunity to engage in sexual innuendo to waken in Kate the desire he feels for her. As *Shrew* is a marriage play, not a courtship play like the other early comedies, Petruchio stresses the physical, sexual aspect of their marriage in both his language and his actions, kissing Kate at their wedding so passionately that "all the church did echo" and kissing her thereafter when things work out to his satisfaction. When he wins the wager at the end, through her cooperation, he kisses her and they go off to consummate their marriage, to the envy of the others: "Come Kate, we'll to bed. / We three are married, but you two are sped."[i] (V, ii, 185-86)

David Daniell notes that Petruchio is acting a role he has devised to cure Kate of her shrewishness: "In all his dealing with her, he acts out a character and a set of situations which present her with a mirror of herself and in particular her high-spirited violence and her sense of being out in the cold and deprived." Daniell observes, "The direction of the play, for Katherine and Petruchio, is towards marriage as a rich, shared sanity."[3]

Petruchio out-Kates Kate in his outrageous behavior at their wedding, as Gremio reports:

*A bridegroom, say you? 'Tis a groom*[ii] *indeed.*
*A grumbling groom, and that the girl shall find.*
Tranio: *Curster than she? Why, 'tis impossible.* (III, ii, 150–52)

Petruchio forgoes the wedding feast to take Kate to his home, where surly servants, hunger, and cold await her, along with a wedding night of wakefulness and enforced chastity. Although Kate is irked by his protestations that his behavior is "under name of perfect love" (IV, iii, 12), she perceives how Petruchio mirrors her former behavior of cursing and violence. Being intelligent, Katherina learns quickly. If Petruchio is playing a role, she can do likewise. On the trip back to her home, she agrees with him that day is night and the sun the moon, and she greets old Vincentio as a "budding virgin" when Petruchio so designates him. Actress Fiona Shaw, a memorable Kate in 1987, points out that Kate takes up the challenge here because Petruchio gives her the choice, another first for her in her new life with him.[4] Theodore Weiss observes that "Petruchio has

[i] worn out (by their selfish wives) [ii] low class servant

helped her to discover how to act, that is, how to be an 'actor' and so herself. She now knows how to play, how, by not taking herself too seriously and so being submerged in herself, to be free of her own fiercely limited rigors and her self-concern. . . . Petruchio has taught her how to transform violence, the product of her frustration, into useful strength and pleasure, best of all gaiety."[5]

The society in which Kate finds herself an alien is a materialistic one that values surface appearances. Their emphasis on clothing Petruchio reduces to absurdity when he turns up for his wedding in what today might be termed "grunge." "To me she's married, not unto my clothes," he remarks, following with a metaphor comparing clothing and sexual intercourse:

*Could I repair what she will wear*[i] *in me*
*As I can change these poor accoutrements,*
*'Twere well for Kate and better for myself.* (III, ii, 115–18)

There seems to be an inordinate emphasis on eating and drinking among the citizens of Padua, and their materialism is satirized in old Gremio's detailed inventory of the furnishings of his house and farm, all of which, because of his advanced age, will be Bianca's very soon if she chooses him for a husband.

Kate's final speech has caused furious debate. Is it to be taken literally? A 1998 production that did so at the Shaw Theatre in London was booed in the theater and excoriated in the reviews. Over a hundred years earlier, in 1897, George Bernard Shaw said of that speech: "No man with any decency of feeling can sit it out in the company of a woman without being extremely ashamed of the lord-of-creation moral implied in the wager and the speech put into the woman's own mouth."[6] Daniell finds that "Marriage is addition, not subtraction: it is a sad let-down if the dazzling action of the play produces only a female wimp. But at the end of the play she shows that she shares with Petruchio an understood frame for both their lives."[7] Michael Billington of the *Guardian*, reviewing a modern-dress 1978 Royal Shakespeare Company production, called the play "barbaric and disgusting."

In her final speech, says Margaret Webster, Katherina is not "a groveling creature, fatuously exalting the male sex in general.

[i] that is, wear out

Her lines are filled with delicious irony, by no means lost on Petruchio, in their delicate overpraising of a husband's virtue." The words "serve, love, and obey" Katherine pronounces as if in quotes "for Petruchio's ears and ours." At the end, states Webster, "the two come together in a beautifully negotiated, not an imposed, peace."[8] Productions of the 1980s and 1990s almost always presented Kate's final speech as irony. In the Royal Shakespeare Company presentation in 1987, Fiona Shaw "emphasized Kate's resistance to what she did not understand and her self-protective reluctance to give very much of herself. Their relationship was founded on a love that grew in tandem with a mutual respect."[9] Shaw describes her approach to the speech, which has aroused so much controversy: Petruchio doesn't know what she will say, but he has faith in her, she believes. At the line, "My hand is ready," she wipes the crumbs off it, and offers it to him, not in resignation but in confidence. He shakes her hand, "an equal partner in a marriage whose intertwined fingers signaled an intelligent peace."[10]

Petruchio wins in the end, says Anne Barton, because he is able to show Katherina "both the unloveliness of the false personality she has adopted and the emotional truth of the self she has submerged. . . . The integrated and quietly confident Kate who wins Petruchio's wager for him at the end of the comedy is a woman who has discovered and come to terms with her own genuine nature."[11]

### *The Comedy of Errors*—Adriana

In *The Comedy of Errors*, even though the characterization is sketchy, Adriana as an older sister seems dependent on Luciana, confiding in her and seeking her advice, although contesting it. When they enter the play at the beginning of act two, Adriana is complaining about her husband to her sister, and their conversation in this early comedy is indicative of Shakespeare's depiction of topics of interest to women. In some ways Adriana is the stereotypical medieval shrew, as depicted by Noah's wife in the mystery plays. In other ways she is a modern wife who disparages her husband for his infidelity but who really cares about him. It is clear that the sisters are close and would have been brought up together, for Luciana, who is single, lives with her sister and brother-in-law. Adriana's insecurity is revealed in a rhymed passage as she asks Luciana (and herself) whether her husband, Antipholus, may have strayed to women more attractive in age, looks, conversation, or dress, but she puts the blame for her loss on him:

*Hath homely age th'alluring beauty took*
*From my poor cheek? Then he hath wasted*[i] *it.*
*Are my discourses dull? Barren my wit?*
*If voluble and sharp discourse be marred,*
*Unkindness blunts it more than marble hard.*
*Do their gay vestments his affections bait?*
*That's not my fault, he's master of my state.*[ii]
*What ruins are in me that can be found*
*By him not ruined? Then is he the ground*
*Of my defeatures*[iii]*; my decay'ed fair*
*A sunny look of his would soon repair.* (II, i, 89–99)

Arguing for equality, Adriana asks regarding men, "Why should their liberty than ours be more?" Luciana gives a stock reply, "Because their business still lies out o'door" (10–11) and continues by arguing for the world order, in which men are "masters to their females." Both sisters are spirited in expressing their contrasting points of view, with Adriana commenting, on her sister's world order speech, "This servitude makes you to keep unwed," to which Luciana replies, "Not this, but troubles of the marriage bed," that is, the example of her sister's marriage (26–27). But by the end of the scene it is apparent that Adriana, to relieve her anxieties, relies on her sister as listener if not as advisor.

In the final scene, Adriana admits to nagging her husband about "some love that drew him oft from home":

*It was the copy of our conference,*
*In bed he slept not for my urging it,*
*At board he fed not for my urging it,*
*Alone, it was the subject of my theme;*
*In company I often glanced at it;*
*Still did I tell him it was vile and bad.*
Abbess: *And thereof came it that the man was mad.* (V, i, 62–68)

[i] (a) literal (b) laid waste to [ii] wealth [iii] ruins

While the abbess blames Antipholus's bizarre behavior on Adriana, Luciana defends her sister: "She never reprehended him but mildly, / When he demeaned himself rough, rude, and wildly" (V, i, 87–88). All is resolved in the end: Adriana is reunited with her husband, Luciana will marry his twin, and the abbess proves to be the twins' long-lost mother.

*The Merry Wives of Windsor*—Margaret Page and Alice Ford

In *The Merry Wives of Windsor*, the only play in the canon about middle-class family life, women manipulate the plot. Into the small town of Windsor, with local characters like the parson, the doctor, and the justice, arrives a stranger, Sir John Falstaff. The fat knight, who wriggled out of every tight situation in the *King Henry IV* plays, will here be outwitted by two wives going about their everyday life in the community.

According to a rumor, which seems to date from 1702, a hundred years after the play was first printed in Quarto, Queen Elizabeth wished to see a play about Falstaff in love, and Shakespeare wrote it in fourteen days. The title page of the 1602 Quarto states that it was "acted . . . before her Majestie and elsewhere." Falstaff had been a favorite with audiences of Shakespeare's *King Henry IV* plays, where he had the cleverest dialogue and maneuvered many jests and plots—like the robbery at Gad's Hill in Part One. There is no known source for *The Merry Wives*, but women outwitting men is a staple plot of the medieval fabliaux, of which Chaucer's "The Merchant's Tale" is an example.

In *The Merry Wives* Sir John inexplicably finds himself in Windsor, the town surrounding the castle of Queen Elizabeth I. Being short of funds and learning that both Ford and Page are well heeled, Falstaff decides to woo their wives, who he believes control the purse strings. He sends an identical love letter to both of them, which they immediately compare, and decide on revenge. The play's plot consists of their revenge, three farcical incidents they devise to discomfort and embarrass the fat knight. Falstaff's lines are only about half as clever as those in the *Henry* plays, but Alice and Margaret assume his former wit in their own dialogue, like Alice's comic hyperbole describing Falstaff's weight: "What tempest, I trow," she asks, "threw this whale, with so many tuns of oil in his belly, ashore at Windsor? How shall I be revenged on him? I think the best way were to entertain him with hope, till the wicked fire of lust have melted him in his own grease" (II, i, 56-60).

At other times, Falstaff's flowery, euphuistic speech, with its balance, allusions, and "unnatural natural history," is contrasted with the forthright remarks of the two women. Wooing Alice and promising her the title of "Lady" provokes her response, "I should be a pitiful lady."

> Falstaff: *Let the court of France show me such another. I see how thy eye would emulate the diamond: thou hast the right arched-beauty of the brow that becomes the ship-tire, the tire-valiant, or any tire of Venetian admittance.*[i]
> Alice: *A plain kerchief, Sir John: my brows become nothing else, nor that well neither.* (III, iii, 46–54)

Prunella Scales, a memorable Margaret Page in the BBC Time Life television production, comments on the challenge the prose presents to actors: "The thick, good-quality homespun prose . . . lavishly embroidered with sixteenth-century idioms and clichés and perfectly suited to Elizabethan Windsor. . . . need[s] actors who are prepared to research their speeches . . . and have the skill and comic technique to deliver the lines so that they sound natural and clear to a modern audience. Given such actors, the lines can come out as fresh and funny as in any popular modern comedy."[12]

When the women are alone together some of their prose takes a bawdy turn, as in their discussion of the identical letters they received from Falstaff. Margaret comments,

> *I warrant he hath a thousand of these letters, writ with blank space for different names (sure, more) and these are of the second edition. He will print them, out of doubt; for he cares not what he puts into the press, when he would put us two. I had rather be a giantess, and lie under Mount Pelion.*[ii] (II, i,66-71)

The farcical incidents, the diverse array of characters that inhabit Windsor and its surrounds, the stylish prose and the fractured English filled with malapropisms that somehow

[i] three elaborate headdresses [ii] "press" and "lie under" are slang for intercourse; in mythology, giants tried to pile Mt. Pelion on Mt. Ossa

manage to be obscene—all are presented against a background of realistic town life. The men are concerned with hunting, with money, and with dining; the women with such home matters as the washing and bleaching of clothes, feeding the family and guests, and caring for the children. If there is a marriageable daughter, like Anne Page, there are suitors to be considered. (Anne has three, one urged by each parent and one she has chosen.) Youngsters' schooling must be monitored, a task Margaret Page assumes. She visits the local schoolmaster Parson Evans and listens to her son William parse and conjugate his Latin (with obscene interpretations from the doyenne of malapropism, Mistress Quickly, undeterred by her ignorance of Latin).

Although the two wives share friendship and interests, their relationships with their husbands differ. George Page is easy-going, accepting, and enjoys life; Frank Ford is nervous and suspicious—a hint that his wife may be unfaithful sends him into a paroxysm of anger. Two of the farcical incidents deal with his unfounded jealousy directed against Falstaff. Although there is no actual source for *The Merry Wives*, a number of stories existed in which a lover unwittingly tells a husband of an affair with his wife, something Ford is hoping to learn when he disguises himself as Master Brook.

It is in their enjoyment of each other's company that Alice and Margaret are such an appealing pair. There is no competition or jealousy between them in their lively manipulation of the situations that will discomfort and (they hope) discourage Falstaff. To imply in his letter that they might be receptive to his advances they find insulting: "What doth he think of us?" they ask, justifying their treatment of him.

In the first of two incidents, Falstaff no sooner arrives at Ford's house to begin his wooing when news comes that Ford is on his way home, forcing Falstaff to flee. The women hide him in a huge basket covered with dirty linen, an Elizabethan laundry list that Falstaff recounts to the audience: "foul shirts and smocks, socks, foul stockings, greasy napkins . . . the rankest compound of villainous smell that ever offended nostril" (III, v, 80–86). The buck-basket is carried to the "whiteners" (bleachers of linens) and the contents, including Falstaff, dumped into a stream. The second time he escapes by cross-dressing. The "fat woman of Brainford" has left a gown in which Alice and Margaret dress Falstaff with a fringed hat and a muffler. Suspecting that she is a witch, Ford has forbidden the fat woman to come to his house, threatening to beat her, as he does upon meeting Falstaff so dressed.

The third device of Mistresses Ford and Page is a country celebration of "Herne the Hunter," the kind of show that often concluded a play intended for presentation both at court and in the public playhouse. *A Midsummer Night's Dream* and *Love's Labour's Lost* include such finales. When Falstaff arrives at the legendary Herne's oak for a third assignation with the two women, the horns of Herne are placed on his head, and fairies pinch him and burn him with their tapers as a cure for his lust. In the show written by Parson Evans, William's schoolchildren friends and his sister Anne are the fairies, Mistress Quickly is the unlikely Queen of the Fairies, and Pistol a hobgoblin. The children playing the fairies (like those in *A Midsummer Night's Dream*) probably were recruited from a private theater. These theaters supported entire companies of children, like St. Paul's Boys, formed from the choir of St. Paul's Cathedral.[13] Two of the show's adult participants, French doctor Caius, Margaret's choice for Anne, and Squire Slender, George's choice, by prearrangement have plotted to steal away with their daughter and get married. But Anne outwits them both and elopes with her choice, Fenton, who is forgiven by the parents, and Margaret Page invites all, including Falstaff, to dinner:

> *Good husband, let us every one go home,*
> *And laugh this sport o'er by a country fire,*
> *Sir John and all.* (V, v, 235–37)

## Notes

[1] Penelope Mortimer, "The Taming of the Shrew," in *Shakespeare in Perspective*, ed. Roger Sales, 197.

[2] Margaret Webster, *Shakespeare Without Tears*, 143.

[3] David Daniell, "The Good Marriage," in *Shakespeare: Early Comedies*, ed. Pamela Mason, 28–29.

[4] Carol Rutter, *Clamorous Voices*, 24.

[5] Theodore Weiss, *The Breath of Clowns and Kings*, 68.

[6] G. B. Shaw, *Shaw on Shakespeare*, ed. Edwin Wilson, 188.

[7] Daniell, "The Good Marriage," 129.

[8] Webster, *Shakespeare Without Tears*, 143.

[9] Pamela Mason, "Recent Productions," in *Shakespeare: Early Comedies*, 135.

[10] Rutter, *Clamorous Voices*, 24.

[11] Anne Barton, "The Taming of the Shrew," Riverside ed., 107.

[12] Prunella Scales, "The Merry Wives," in *Shakespeare in Perspective*, 146.

[13] Muriel C. Bradbrook, "London Pageantry and Lawyers' Theater," in *Shakespeare's Rough Magic*, ed. Peter Erickson and Coppelia Kahn, 259.

# CHAPTER SIX: ROMANCES

*The Winter's Tale, All's Well That Ends Well,* and *Cymbeline*

*The Winter's Tale*—Hermione and Paulina

In the opening scenes of *The Winter's Tale*, Queen Hermione, wife of Leontes, King of Sicilia, appears in an enviable position—she is secure in her marriage, the pregnant mother of a young son, and a witty, vivacious hostess to visiting King Polixenes. Suddenly everything changes. Her husband, madly jealous, accuses her of adultery with Polixenes and throws her into prison. However, the threats and dangers of the alien world in which she finds herself only strengthen Hermione's resolve. Like other heroines faced with danger in the comedies, she discovers resources within herself and attempts to resolve the situation. When she gives birth, the baby is taken from her, and Leontes orders the "bastard" destroyed. In act three, scene two, a formal trial is held by Leontes, in order to "proceed in justice."

The indictment is read by an officer: she is charged with "high treason" for committing adultery with Polixenes, and for conspiring against Leontes's life with courtier Camillo, whom she helped escape. None of this is true. Hermione defends herself in a long speech, very different in style from her earlier, light-hearted remarks. In clear, direct language she rationally develops her argument. First, since she is alone, allowed no witnesses, she realizes the futility of her defense, but she hopes that "powers divine" are watching (which anticipates the Oracle). Next, she is fighting not for herself but for her honor and as a legacy to her children, and third, she specifically denies each charge in turn. Leontes, both the prosecutor and the judge, insists that she is lying and pronounces a sentence of death.

Hermione's defense so far has been factual; she now appeals to emotions and describes her treatment. Death holds no threat for her because she seeks it, having lost all in life that gave her joy, Leontes's favor, her son, and the baby, who:

*Starred most unluckily, is from my breast—*
*The innocent milk in it most innocent mouth—*
*Haled out to murder. Myself on every post*
*Proclaimed a strumpet: with immodest hatred*
*The child-bed privilege denied, which 'longs*
*To women of all fashion. Lastly, hurried*
*Here, to this place, i' th' open air, before*
*I have got strength of limit.* (III, ii, 99–106)

She calls upon the Oracle from the Temple of Apollo to decide her fate. While waiting for it to be read, she reminds the court that "the Emperor of Russia was my father"; if he were still alive, and could see her misery, she hopes he would act with "pity, not revenge" (119-23). The Oracle announces that she is innocent and Leontes "a jealous tyrant." Leontes's on-the-spot repentance is to no avail, for Hermione faints, is whisked away by Paulina, and pronounced dead.

The relationship of Paulina and Hermione is deep and lasting, as well as fortunate for the accused Hermione, who has no one except another woman to turn to in the hostile male world that surrounds her and threatens her with death. Paulina is aggressive as well as tender when she insists on seeing Hermione in the jail where she has given birth, and she is resourceful in convincing the jailer to let her depart with the baby. She has her own idiom, clear, direct and simple. As she says, she will use her tongue to trumpet her anger, but as the last two lines indicate, she shows wisdom as well:

*He*[i] *must be told on't, and he shall: the office*
*Becomes a woman best, I'll take 't upon me:*
*If I prove honey-mouthed, let my tongue blister,*
*And never to my red-looked anger be*
*The trumpet any more. . . .*
*I'll show' t the king, and undertake to be*
*Her advocate to th' loud'st. We do not know*

[i] the king

*How he may soften at the sight o' th' child:*
*The silence often of pure innocence*
*Persuades, when speaking fails.* (II, ii, 31–42)

Nothing can shake Paulina's loyalty to Hermione and her insistence to the maddened Leontes that the child is his. When she continues to harangue him on this subject, he threatens to have her burned, but to no effect, for she turns his threat into tyranny on his part and martyrdom for herself, saying that the fault of a woman burned at the stake is not with her but with her condemner:

Leontes: *I'll ha' thee burnt.*
Paulina: *I care not:*
*It is an heretic that makes the fire,*
*Not she which burns in 't.* (II, iii, 113–15)

Paulina, who becomes a widow when her husband loses his life saving the baby's, resembles the medieval shrew in some respects. Although she may have a "trumpet" for a tongue, she also knows when to keep silent. At Hermione's trial, Paulina says nothing, but when Hermione faints on hearing the Oracle, Paulina declares, "This news is mortal to the queen: look down / And see what death is doing" (III, ii, 148–49). She spirits Hermione away, only to return and announce that she is dead. Being Paulina, she takes twenty-six lines to deliver the news, as she castigates Leontes as a fool and a murderer. Paulina's voice is one we will hear again in the plays, outspoken, direct, and shrewd, a quality echoed by characters like Emilia in *Othello.*

Her main occupation during the sixteen-year interlude before the action resumes in Bohemia with Perdita, has been to continually remind the penitent Leontes of the worth of Hermione and of his reprehensible actions, that as he admits, "Destroyed the sweetest companion that e'er man / Bred his hopes out of." Paulina replies, rubbing salt in the wound:

*True, too true, my lord:*
*If, one by one, you wedded all the world,*
*Or from the all that are, took something good,*
*To make a perfect woman, she you killed*
*Would be unparalleled.* (V, i, 12–16)

At last satisfied with Leontes's repentance, Paulina stage-manages the magical final scene, in which the "statue" of Hermione is brought to life. "She comes alive," says Rosalie Colie, "because she can forgive, comes alive when she does because Leontes is ready to receive at her hands what no man has a right to expect, the forgiveness that fulfills the utmost selfishness of his dreams."[1] Only Paulina, not even the audience, has the knowledge that Hermione lives, and over the years Paulina sustains her until judging the right time to restore Hermione to Leontes. The stage effect is especially moving as Paulina calls the "statue" to life:

*'Tis time: descend: be stone no more: approach:*
*Strike all that look upon with marvel. Come:*
*I'll fill your grave up: stir: nay, come away:*
*Bequeath to Death your numbness: for from him*
*Dear life redeems you.* (V, iii, 99–103)

In the 1980 BBC Time-Life production, Anna Calder-Marshall could perhaps show more backbone as Hermione; even in her courtroom defense she is somewhat subdued. But Margaret Tyzak is perfect as the outspoken Paulina. In her scenes, she literally rules the small screen, strong and assertive with the courtiers, who shrink from her sharp tongue, sympathetic with Hermione, accusatory with Leontes, and totally in command in the finale.

## *All's Well that Ends Well*—Helena

Helena in *All's Well that Ends Well* is Shakespeare's New Woman. She is educated, resourceful, self-aware, determined, energetic, eloquent, and persuasive, a woman who identifies her goals and takes advantage of the opportunities to achieve them. She is also young and beautiful. Her intelligence guides her behavior as she encounters a disparate array of persons old and young, honorable and dishonorable. Above all she understands the man she loves, whom she maneuvers into marrying her in act one. Immediately after the ceremony he rejects her and sets seemingly impossible conditions for accepting her as his wife. How she meets these conditions is the story of *All's Well.*

If the plot sounds like a medieval folktale (itself a descendent of such ancient prophecy-come-true stories as "Oedipus"), it is.

Shakespeare found the story in William Painter's "The Palace of Pleasure," taken from Boccaccio, a favorite source for Chaucer, whose "loathly lady" Wyf of Bath's tale is a variation. Shakespeare, newly discovered as the first feminist, transforms his heroine from Giletta to Helena, whose character and actions the audience identifies with and cheers on through every step of her journey.

Of all Shakespeare's heroines, Helena is the most sexually aware; she recognizes and expresses her desire for Bertram in physical terms and is explicit when she describes to him (in public) her satisfaction with their single sexual encounter, which lasts only an hour but results in her pregnancy, another achievement. Like other Shakespearean comedies, *All's Well that Ends Well* begins on a serious note as the characters enter dressed "all in black." The count of Rossillion, father of Bertram, has just died, and the young count, secretly beloved of Helena, is off to Paris to the court of the perilously ill king. Bertram's mother, the countess, wishes that Helena's father, a famous physician attendant at court, had not recently died. Helena has only one sentence in the general mourning, until all leave the stage, and then she is given a serious soliloquy, followed by a dialogue with Parolles, Bertram's companion, who Helena realizes is "a notorious liar," a "fool," and a "coward."

Barbara Everett points out that Helena is the only one of Shakespeare's comedy heroines to be given "genuinely introspective" soliloquies, which she needs, being "inward" with a "quality of female self-containedness with which Shakespeare seems to have been more and more concerned in the mature comedies."[2] Her first soliloquy expresses her love for Bertram and her realization that she, being lowly born, is "not in his sphere," the same metaphor Polonius uses in warning Ophelia against Hamlet. Bertram is unattainable: "The hind[i] that would be mated by the lion / Must die for love." The lion is a symbol of royalty, representing the king of the beasts. But like so many of the images in this play, there are sexual overtones, as Helena sees Bertram's strength and virility as lionlike. She continues to dwell on his physical attributes: "his arch'ed brows, his hawking eye, his curls" are drawn in her heart, along with "every line and trick of his sweet favour."[ii] Up to this point, she seems resigned to worshipping him in her mind as her "idolatrous fancy."

[i] female deer [ii] face

But she is encouraged to find she can hold her own with the despicable Parolles. He approaches her with a "dirty mouth," typical of the misogynist he is: "Are you meditating on virginity?" She ignores his question and asks an insulting one of her own, couched in terms of warfare and aware that this braggart is not the war hero he claims to be: "Man is enemy to virginity; how may we barricado it against him? . . . Unfold to us some warlike resistance." Parolles continues, using military terms for obscene references to the sexual act: "Man setting down before you will undermine you and blow you up."[i] He argues in behalf of "loss of virginity" until Helena asks another question, a thought or even a plan forming in her mind: "How might one do, sir, to lose it to her own liking?" Parolles' reply does not deter Helena: "Marry, ill, to like him that ne'er it likes."[ii] She makes use of Parolles to send Bertram a message couched in sonnet terms:

*There*[iii] *shall your master have a thousand loves,*
*A mother, and a mistress, and a friend,*
*A phoenix, captain, and an enemy,*
*A guide, a goddess, and a sovereign,*
*A counsellor, a traitress, and a dear.* (I, i, 162–66)

As Parolles departs, he prophetically advises Helena to "Get thee a good husband, and use[iv] him as he uses thee."

Helena's next soliloquy, in rhyme, is more determined than her earlier rumination:

*Our remedies oft in ourselves do lie,*
*Which we ascribe to heaven. The fated sky*
*Gives us free scope, only doth backward pull*
*Our slow designs when we ourselves are dull.* (I, i, 212–15)

Since our destiny gives us "free scope" only we can hold ourselves back; nothing is impossible. "Who ever strove / To show her merit that did miss her love?" Her project is to travel to Paris to cure the king (as well as to see Bertram) and her intentions are firm: "The King's disease—my project may deceive me, / But my intents are fixed, and will not leave me" (I, i, 222–25).

[i] that is, in pregnancy [ii] one would not do well to lose it to one who cares nothing for it [iii] (a) Paris (b) her virginity [iv] that is, sexually

Helena's declaration of love for Bertram is overheard by a steward, who reports this to Bertram's mother, the countess of Rossillion. Sympathetic to Helena, whom she has raised and educated as a daughter, she asks three times whether Helena loves Bertram. She finally confesses that she does:

*My friends*[i] *were poor, but honest; So's my love.*
*Be not offended, for it hurts not him*
*That he is loved of me. . . .*
*Nor would I have him till I do deserve him,*
*Yet never know how that desert should be.* (I, iii, 190–95)

It is a truthful, well-balanced, direct answer, neither humble nor presumptuous and not ruling out the possibility that she might "deserve him." When the countess asks if she believes she can cure the king with prescriptions left her by her physician father, Helena replies with confidence, "Ay, madam, knowingly."

At Paris, Helena is able to persuade the king that she holds the cure to his illness in her prescriptions. She stakes her life on her cure, and the king agrees to try it, which "ministers thine own death if I die." Helena is not so carried away by his consent that she fails to ask in advance for her reward if she is successful: "Then shalt thou give me with thy kingly hand / What husband in thy power I will command" (II, i, 192–93). Completely cured, the king will now uphold his end of the bargain and calls in "a youthful parcel / Of noble bachelors." E. A. J. Honigmann terms it "a beauty parade of young lords" that "reverses sexual prerogatives, for it is usually the ladies who are on show, the men who select."[3] Although the first lord indicates he will grant her suit, the next two reject her, and she, turning down the fourth as "too young," chooses Bertram, addressing him in terms that are so endearing that no one except Bertram could fail to assent:

*I dare not say I take you, but I give*
*Me and my service, ever whilst I live,*
*Into your guiding power.* [to the king]: *This is the man.*
(II, iii, 102–104)

Bertram rejects Helena because she is poor and low-born: "A poor physician's daughter my wife!" The king replies with an argument out of folk-tale as Chaucer expresses it: "True gentilesse[ii] cometh from God alone."

[i] relatives [ii] nobility of character

*From lowest place when virtuous things proceed,*
*The place is dignified by th'doer's deed.* (II, iii, 125-26)

"She is young, wise, fair," her inheritance from nature, the king reminds Bertram. "Virtue and she is her own dower; honor and wealth from me" (131, 143-44). Since her brief speech to Bertram, Helena, wisely, has said nothing; she has let the king speak in her behalf. Now, again wisely, she magnanimously tells the king that she will not claim marriage to Bertram: "That you are well restored, my lord, I'm glad / Let the rest go" (II, iii, 147–48). Does Helena know that the king will insist? She takes risks throughout her journey to her goal, and this may be one of them. As she hoped, the king is firm: "My honor's at the stake. . . . Here, take her hand, / Proud, scornful boy. . . . Check thy contempt. . . . Or I will throw thee from my care for ever." Bertram asks the king's pardon, finding that

*she, which late*
*Was in my nobler thoughts most base, is now*
*The prais'ed of the King; who, so ennobled,*
*Is as 'twere born so.* (II, iii, 149–73)

Not only is Helena suddenly elevated in social status, she is now rich—the king will give her an estate equal to (if not better than) Bertram's and announces that the marriage ceremony will be performed that night.

Despite the warnings against Parolles by Lafew and other lords, Bertram still employs as confidant and companion the man his mother says "corrupts" the "well-deriv'ed nature" of her son (III, ii, 88). Parolles encourages Bertram to run away to the wars in Tuscany and Bertram (who will use Helena's dowry from the king to "furnish" him for the wars) invites Parolles to "advise me." Parolles is like the evil angel of the morality plays (and Marlowe's *Doctor Faustus*) who struggles against the good angel, Helena, for possession of Bertram (II, iii, 286, 90).

After the ceremony, Bertram orders Helena back to Rossillion, and she who can argue so persuasively quietly accepts his wishes. In fact, she is so obedient and humble as to make him uncomfortable, "Come, come, no more of that. . . . Let that go. My haste is very great. Farewell; hie home" (II, v, 77). But Helena lingers; "like a timorous thief," she "would steal / What law does vouch mine own. . . . Strangers and foes do sunder and not kiss." He ignores her request for a kiss: "I pray you, stay not, but in haste to horse" (II, v, 80, 86). Is she role-playing, enacting the kind of wife she thinks Bertram wants? His attentions to Diana—whose take-charge manner is like Helena's—indicate that he does not know what kind of wife he wants.

Helena has returned to the countess when Bertram's letter arrives stating the conditions, which he claims will be "never," under which she can "call me husband": she must get the ring from his finger and "show me a child begotten of thy body that I am father to." The countess is outraged: "I do wash his name out of my blood / And thou art all my child" (III, ii, 67–68). Helena, she says, deserves better: "a lord that twenty such rude boys might tend upon" (81). But like any mother, the countess makes excuses for her "rude boy"—he is corrupted by bad company (Parolles). Helena in her next soliloquy also blames someone other than Bertram; she herself has driven him to the wars and worries that the body she loves will be harmed:

*Poor lord, is't I*
*That chase thee from thy country, and expose*
*Those tender limbs of thine to the event*[i]
*Of the none-sparing war?. . .*
*Whoever charges on his forward breast,*
*I am the caitiff*[ii] *that do hold him to't.* (III, ii, 102–14)

As he has vowed not to return home "'till I have no wife," she will leave, again comparing herself to a thief, with echoes of the denied kiss: "With the dark, poor thief, I'll steal away" (129). She becomes a pilgrim to St. Jaques le Grand, travels by way of Florence, and arrives there just in time to witness the victory parade of the Florentines, led by Bertram as general. Seeking out the house where the pilgrims stay, she meets her landlady, a widow, and her daughter, Diana. The news about Bertram's rejection of his wife has reached them, and the widow not only pities the woman, but remarks that "This young maid might do her / A shrewd turn if she pleased"(III, v, 66–67). Helena is quick to see how this might serve her aim to fulfill the conditions set by Bertram: "Maybe the amorous Count solicits her / In the unlawful purpose?" (69). She invites them to dinner at her expense, and her plot is under way.

[i] outcome [ii] wretch

With the exception of Bertram and Parolles, everyone responds favorably to Helena and trusts her. The king's bounty means that Helena can materially reward the women's trust with a "purse of gold." Her plan is to have Diana consent to an assignation with Bertram, demand the ring he wears with another to be exchanged in its place, and at the time of the encounter "delivers me to fill the time, / Herself most chastely absent"(III, vii, 33–34). Their meeting is to last only an hour, in the dark, neither speaking. The "bed trick" or the "substitute bride" was a device of the folk tale, and Shakespeare also uses it in *Measure for Measure*. In carrying out their assignments, the widow and Diana, notes Honigmann, being "remarkably business-like, help to suggest that Helena's efficiency is not necessarily unfeminine, and the four ladies together, opposing the irresponsible Bertram and Parolles, tip the whole play firmly towards a feminine point of view."[4]

Inspired no doubt by Helena, Diana shows herself in the seduction scene to be more than a match for Bertram. He may have expected swooning acquiescence, but what he gets are pointed reminders of his duty to his wife, put-downs, and turns of his argument against himself. When she asks for his ring, he claims it is "an honor 'longing to our house / Bequeath'ed down from many ancestors." She cleverly picks up his words, repeats them incrementally, and applies them to her chastity:

*Mine honor's such a ring;*
*My chastity's the jewel of our house*
*Bequeath'ed down from many ancestors.* (IV, ii, 42–47)

After Bertram departs and the encounter has been arranged, Diana reflects that her mother "told me just how he would woo / As if she sat in's heart. She says all men / Have the like oaths. He had sworn to marry me / When his wife's dead" (69–72). His oath will fuel Helena's next transaction—the false report of her death at the shrine of Saint Jaques le Grand: "there residing, the tenderness of her nature became as a prey to her grief; in fine, made a groan of her last breath, and now she sings in heaven," says one of the French lords. His companion recounts that Bertram "hath perverted a young gentlewoman here in Florence, of a most chaste renown, and this night he fleshes his will[i] in the spoil of her honor" (IV, iii, 49–50, 12–15).

[i] sexual inclination

That same night Parolles is revealed for what he is—a braggart, a liar, a disparager of his fellow soldiers (including Bertram) and a traitor to the flag under which he enlisted. His own comrades trick him into believing he is captured by the enemy; blindfolded, he betrays them all to save his own skin. Bertram, convinced, leaves his evil angel but is yet to accept his good angel, who with Diana and the widow, is making her way to Rossillion, where the king also is headed. The two scenes with the women indicate their bonding as they express their faith in her: "You never had a servant to whose trust / Your business was more welcome," says the widow. Helena confides in them what she will announce later in public—her satisfaction with her sexual encounter with Bertram:

*O strange men!*
*That can such sweet use make of what they hate*[i]
*When saucy trusting of the cozened*[ii] *thoughts*
*Defiles the pitchy night.* (IV, iv, 21–24)

There may be tough going ahead for them, she cautions, but she promises that "All's well that ends well."

The stage is set for the final scene in which all will be ended well, despite some threatening moments. Helena's plan is for Diana to confront Bertram with his promise of marriage should he be widowed. Bertram tries to lie his way out of the charge, claiming she seduced him. In a stressful situation, Diana performs well, probably coached by Helena. When Diana asks for the return of the ring on his finger, which she says was given to him in bed, the king recognizes it as his, a present to Helena. He commands that Diana explain where she got the ring, and her replies are enigmatic, even when he threatens imprisonment and death. She calls for bail; Helena, pregnant, enters in answer to Diana's riddle: "one that's dead is quick"[iii] (V, iii, 297). Bertram finally sees the light, and when Helena says she is "but the shadow of a wife you see, / The name and not the thing," he exclaims that she is "Both, both"—the wife in reality and entitled to the name. He asks her pardon. Helena's reply is a comment on his sexual performance: "O my good lord, when I was like this maid / I found you wondrous kind.[iv] She produces his ring,

[i] that is, herself [ii] tricked [iii] (a) alive (b) pregnant [iv] (a) gentle (b) natural

repeats the conditions he set, which have been met: "This is done. / Will you be mine now you are doubly won?" Bertram promises the king that once everything is explained clearly "I'll love her dearly, ever, ever dearly" (V, iii, 301–10).

Is Bertram worth it? He is, to Helena. In his defense it might be noted that everyone speaks well of him. He is young and inexperienced; as his mother says when he goes off to the court as a ward of the king: "'Tis an unseasoned courtier." She asks the older Lafew to advise him, but Bertram chooses Parolles as his guide, dazzled by his outlandish clothes and fustian language. As sympathetically played by Toby Stephens in his twenties in a Royal Shakespeare Company production, his behavior was consistent with youth and inexperience, not to mention being anxious to throw off the domination of an indulgent mother. As to marriage, he wants what all young people want: to choose for himself. Being young and lacking experience, he may well be telling the truth to Diana in the seduction scene:

*Love is holy,*
*And my integrity n'er knew the crafts*
*That you do charge men with.* (IV, ii, 32–34)

His behavior in the final scene is far from commendable, as he tries to squirm out of the charges against him, but when he affirms to Helena that she is both the name and the reality of a wife to him, the audience, along with Helena, wants to believe him.

### *Cymbeline*—Imogen

Imogen in *Cymbeline* has the resourcefulness that marks Shakespeare's other comedy heroines, but in this late romance the trials she must undergo are far greater. None suffer as she does from a patriarchy that demands a forced marriage and jails her when she refuses, a stepmother who plots to poison her, a husband who accepts a false report of her unfaithfulness and orders her murder, a trip on foot across England (disguised as a boy and starving), a potion that induces inertness believed to be death, undergoing a funeral, and waking on the decapitated body of a man she believes to be her husband. Faithful wife Imogen has the toughness and the intelligence to survive all this, to recognize the villainy that betrayed her and her husband, to force restitution, and to forgive her husband with whom she presumably lives happily and uneventfully ever after.

Favoring a complicated plot, Shakespeare combines the Holinshed history of King Cymbeline, who reigned in England in 33 B.C. with a wager story found in Boccaccio's *Decameron*, novel 9. In the story a man loses a wager on his wife's virtue when his opponent conceals himself in a chest in her chamber at night, then emerges, observes the room, studies her sleeping body, and notes a birthmark. When he reports this to the husband and wins the wager, the husband orders a servant to kill his wife. She escapes disguised as a sailor, and meets the villain, who brags of his ruse where the husband can overhear; the pair are reunited and the villain punished. The play's wicked queen stepmother, who tries to poison Imogen, is from the fairy tale world of *Snow White.* Her oafish son, Cloten, is chosen by the queen and Cymbeline as a husband for Imogen, who defies them and marries Posthumus, so named because his father died before he was born and his mother died in childbirth.

Like many other women in Shakespeare's plays, Imogen has a sharp tongue and spares no one, not even her father the king:

> Cymbeline: *Thou mightst have had the sole son of my queen.*
> Imogen: *O blessed, that I might not: I chose an eagle,*
> *And did avoid a puttock.*[i] (I, ii, 69–71)

She taunts the queen when it is reported that Cloten drew his sword on the banished Posthumus as he departed:

> *he takes his part*
> *To draw upon an exile. O brave sir:*
> *I would they were in Afric both together,*
> *Myself by with a needle, that I might prick*
> *The goer-back.* (I, ii, 96–100)

Her choice of insulting words to describe Cloten to both the king and queen indicates that he preys on others and is a coward who dare not face Posthumus on equal grounds.

Wagerer Iachimo, the villain of the play, bears some resemblance to Iago, another Italian. His malignancy, however, is not motiveless because Iachimo stands to win the wager of money and Imogen's ring worn by banished Posthumus. When

[i] kite, a bird of prey

Iachimo is concealed in Imogen's chamber as she sleeps, he removes her bracelet. On that occasion, he compares himself to Tarquin, but Imogen is no Lucretia, who killed herself rather than face dishonor. Iachimo has falsely reported to Imogen that Posthumus was misbehaving with other women while in Rome, where "he is called / The Briton reveller" (I, vii, 60–61). As does Iago, Iachimo uses salacious and ugly allusions. But Imogen is no Othello either and will not alter her love for Posthumus. Iachimo then confesses his report was false, to test her, and asks that she guard his trunk of jewels in her bedchamber for safekeeping. She agrees. Iachimo will be the "jewel" in the trunk that night.

When faithful servant Pisanio shows Imogen the order from Posthumus for her death for having "played the strumpet in my bed," she immediately recalls Iachimo's account of Posthumus's wild behavior in Rome and suspects she has been replaced in his affections by another woman, some "jay of Italy":

> *Poor I am stale, a garment out of fashion,*
> *And for*[i] *I am richer than to hang by th' walls,*
> *I must be ripped—to pieces with me—O,*
> *Men's vows are women's traitors!* (III. iv, 49–54)

Like "needle" (I, ii, 99), the image is drawn from everyday household activities. Her image here is from clothing—a good discarded garment to be ripped up to make other clothes rather than hung up and used as a cleaning rag. As her hardships increase, Imogen's speech gets tougher, but her allusions are still women-related. In the men's clothing Pisanio provides to disguise her, she is to make her way to Milford Haven on the west coast and present herself to serve Lucius, a Roman who has landed there to collect tribute from Cymbeline. The king, however, prefers fighting to paying. After two nights of traveling, sleeping on the ground, and starving, Imogen still is resolute. Her soliloquy explains that famine makes one "valiant": "Plenty and peace breeds cowards: hardness ever / Of hardiness is mother" (III, vi, 21–22).

By Shakespearean coincidence, the cave where she shelters houses her two long-lost brothers. Struck by their nobility of

[i] because

character, she remarks in an aside that they are the equal of "great men" except that the latter enjoy what she wisely regards as the "nothing-gift of differing multitudes," that is, the worthless adulation of the fickle crowd. They invite her to join them, but she soon falls ill and drinks the "cordial" given her by the queen as a restorative. It is actually a potion (like the one Juliet takes) that induces a deathlike sleep, which the queen's physician brewed to be harmless when he was ordered to prepare a poison for Imogen. Believing Imogen dead, the brothers lay her to rest as they sing a dirge: "Golden lads and girls all must, / As chimney-sweepers come to dust" (IV, ii, 262–63).

When Posthumus receives a feigned report of Imogen's death, he immediately repents having ordered her death and joins the British army to fight for her side rather than for his Roman countrymen:

*so I'll die*
*For thee, O Imogen, even for whom my life*
*Is, every breath, a death.* (V, i, 25–27)

In the final battle, Cymbeline and the Britons prevail, Iachimo is taken prisoner, as is the Roman Lucius, whom Imogen serves as a page. She notices the ring on Iachimo's finger and asks how he obtained it. When Iachimo tells the full story, Posthumus is ready to kill him. The page Posthumus has brushed aside is identified as Imogen, and the play ends with a mass family reunion of husband and wife, father and sons, and father and daughter, the wicked queen having died. Posthumus forgives Iachimo, and Cymbeline pardons everyone.

The role of Imogen is a favorite with actresses, growing as it does in strength through survival. Her dialogue is clear and direct, sparse but exact in imagery and with a toughness that matches its heroine. However, the play is difficult to mount successfully because of the size of the cast and the complications of the plot. Peter Hall directed it with great acclaim for the Royal National Theatre in London in 1988 with Geraldine James impressive as an Imogen determined to win back Posthumus and Tim Pigott-Smith creating a rounded character of the villainous Iachimo as a destroyer of marriages, reminiscent of Iago. But the play is seldom seen outside of England. A visit to

Brooklyn, New York, by the Royal Shakespeare Company in the spring of 1998 was received less than enthusiastically, especially by critics who reviewed the plot rather than the production.

## Notes

[1] Rosalie Colie, *Shakespeare's Living Art*, 281.

[2] Barbara Everett, "Introduction," *All's Well that Ends Well*, 16.

[3] E. A. J. Honigmann, *Myriad-Minded Shakespeare*, 138–39.

[4] Ibid., 93.

# CHAPTER SEVEN: TRAGEDIES

*Julius Caesar, Coriolanus, Hamlet, Othello, Macbeth,* and *King Lear*

## *Julius Caesar*—Calphurnia and Portia

In Shakespeare's tragedies, women are not as prominent as they are in the comedies and romances, nor do they determine the action. Generally they become victims of circumstances beyond their control, although a wrong decision on their part may incur tragedy. In *Julius Caesar* Shakespeare broadens his picture of Roman politics and war by introducing one domestic scene each for his principals, Caesar and Brutus, and by contrasting their wives in the tense atmosphere leading up to the assassination. Calphurnia first appears in act one, when she is directed by Caesar to stand in Antony's way when he competes in the races:

> *for our elders say,*
> *The barren, touch'ed in this holy chase,*
> *Shake off their sterile curse.* (I, ii, 7–9)

A supreme egotist, Caesar blames his wife for their childless marriage. The passage also suggests a less than mutual relationship in the marriage. The night before the assassination Calphurnia's dreams predict Caesar's murder, an incident Shakespeare bases on his source, North's translation of Plutarch's *Lives.* Earlier critics depict Calphurnia's character as fearful, although Plutarch specifically says that "Calphurnia until that time was never given to any fear and superstition." Harley Granville-Barker believes that "Calphurnia is a nervous, fear-haunted creature . . . . desperate and helpless."[1] In act two, scene two, although shaken by her dream and the reports she has heard of the disturbances in the heavens that "blaze forth the death of princes" (31), she is firm in her decision, virtually an order to Caesar: "You shall not stir out of your house today" (9). As a strong woman who sensibly fears the portents and tries to persuade Caesar to avoid danger, her character is more impressive than Barker suggests. Caesar proclaims: "Danger knows full well / That Caesar is more dangerous than he" (44–45) and stubbornly persists in his decision to go to the Senate. Knowing him better perhaps than he knows himself, Calphurnia decides on another tactic, a compliment that carries a warning: "Your wisdom is consumed in confidence." Realizing how important his image is to him, she finally convinces him by advising that he "call it my fear / That keeps you in the house, and not your own" (50–51).

Decius, a conspirator who arrives to accompany Caesar, slyly interprets her dream as favorable and succeeds in disparaging her concern and challenging Caesar with an image of cowardice:

> *it were a mock*
> *Apt to be rendered, for some one to say,*
> *'Break up the Senate, till another time,*
> *When Caesar's wife shall meet with better dreams.'* (II, ii, 96–99)

Caesar joins in the disparagement: "How foolish do your fears seem now Calphurnia" (105). These are his last words to her. In the scene as written, Calphurnia impresses with her concern and her wise advice; Caesar by comparison has no regard or respect for his wife, but goes his own way, foolhardy and blinded by flattery.

Plutarch depicts Portia, the wife of Brutus, as an educated woman, "being excellently well seen in philosophy, loving her husband well, and being of a noble courage."[2] Aware of how troubled Brutus is, she is concerned that he is not sharing his problems with her, as he has done in the past. That she is sensitive to his feelings can be seen in her reply when he says he is not well:

> *No my Brutus,*
> *You have some sick offense within your mind,*
> *Which by the right and virtue of my place*
> *I ought to know of.* (II, i, 266–69)

The daughter of Cato, the famous Stoic, Portia has proved her courage in the Roman fashion by wounding herself in the thigh: "Can I bear that with patience / And not my husband's secrets?" (301–2). She convinces Brutus by her strong and well-reasoned argument that as his wife, with equality in marriage, she is entitled to share his secret:

*Within the bond of marriage, tell me Brutus,*
*Is it excepted I should know no secrets*
*That appertain to you? Am I your self,*
*But as it were in sort, or limitation?*
*To keep with you at meals, comfort your bed,*
*And talk to you sometimes? Dwell I but in the suburbs*[i]
*Of your good pleasure? If it be no more,*
*Portia is Brutus' harlot, not his wife.* (II, i, 280-86)

Brutus having told her about the assassination, she now worries about him and sends their servant Lucius to the Senate House for news (II, iv). Later, during the wars, Brutus learns that she has killed herself in the Stoic tradition when hearing of his defeat. Even though Calphurnia and Portia are minor figures in the play and do not affect the action, by including them Shakespeare not only adds two contrasting female figures in contrasting marriage relationships, but he contributes another facet to the characters of both Caesar and Brutus by depicting them interacting with their wives.

Actresses generally avoid the two women's roles in this play because they are so brief, but in the 1953 film version of the play, both Greer Garson as Calphurnia and Deborah Kerr as Portia turn in convincing and creditable performances, making clear the discord between Caesar and his wife and the mutual affection and regard between Brutus and Portia.

*Coriolanus*—Virgilia and Volumnia

In another Roman tragedy, *Coriolanus*, Virgilia is a wife neglected by her husband, Coriolanus, and dominated by her mother-in-law, Volumnia. When the three are together, Virgilia has little to say, and the conversation is between mother and son discussing a single topic—warfare. As Virgilia displays a distaste for battle and bloodshed, she and Coriolanus seem to have little in common. That she genuinely loves him is apparent in her

[i] where the brothels were located

fears for his safety, and finally—almost at the end of the play—Coriolanus (in exile) declares his love for her.

In a scene original with Shakespeare, Coriolanus's mother and his wife are introduced in a domestic setting reminiscent of other plays where women in an intimate indoor scene discuss men. Here they are speaking of Coriolanus as they await his return from battling the Volsces led by Aufidius at Corioli. The immediate contrast between the two women, besides their ages, is apparent in Volumnia's directness of speech, her dominance of the conversation, and her single subject: her only son, Coriolanus. Like many mothers, she likes to dwell on her role in his upbringing and to take credit for his present success:

> *When yet he was but tender-bodied, and the only son of my womb, when youth with comeliness plucked all gaze his way, when for a day of kings' entreaties, a mother should not sell him an hour from her beholding, I, considering how honor would become such a person . . .was pleased to let him seek danger where he was like to find fame. To a cruel war I sent him.* (I, iii, 5–13)

Virgilia, quieter and more moderate, points out that Coriolanus might have died in that first battle. Volumnia reveals how her life, and through her, that of Coriolanus, are ruled by one thought only—winning glory in war. Had she had a dozen sons, she replies, "I had rather had eleven die nobly for their country than one voluptuously surfeit[i] out of action" (24–25). If she cannot go to war herself, which she should like to have done, her son can fulfill her fantasies. She acts out the fantasy as she describes his bravery in the current battle: "Methinks I see him stamp thus, and call thus: 'Come on, you cowards!'" (32–33). When Virgilia prays that there be no blood, Volumnia calls her a fool and insists:

> *It more becomes a man*
> *Than gilt his trophy. The breasts of Hecuba,*
> *When she did suckle Hector, looked not lovelier*
> *Than Hector's forehead when it spit forth blood*
> *At Grecian sword, contemning.* (I, iii, 40–44)

[i] indulge himself

Her image contrasting a mother's nursing a baby with a war hero's bleeding and showing contempt for his wound is central to the play, an inversion that portrays destruction as preferable to nurturing. This contrast of the domestic world with the world of war and politics will continue, with many allusions to home, nurturing, and family, while the action is concerned with the destruction of war and the treachery of politics. In a way the two women represent these opposite worlds: Virgilia, who in her initial appearance is sewing and will not leave the house until she hears of Coriolanus's safe return, and Volumnia who, unable to go to war herself, has brought up her son to achieve glory in battle. At the climax, the familial tableau of Coriolanus's wife, mother, and son beseeching him to avert war with Rome signals a triumph for the family and a defeat for war hero Coriolanus.

The relationship between Volumnia and Coriolanus has Oedipal overtones, which are apparent in Volumnia's second sentence in the play, addressed to Virgilia: "If my son were my husband, I should freelier rejoice in that absence wherein he won honor than in the embracements of his bed where he would show most love" (I, iii, 2–5). Later in the action, in persuading him to play a role to win the people's vote for Consul, she advises that she would "dissemble" with "honor" if required to do so: "I am in this / Your wife, your son, these Senators, the nobles" (III, ii, 62–65).

Throughout the action, Coriolanus's wife is in the background. She says little, and he rarely addresses her. It is almost as if Virgilia fears him, although she can speak pertly to others when her husband is absent. When Rome is in danger from the Volsces, with whom Coriolanus has joined, the two tribunes who have manipulated his banishment meet Volumnia and Virgilia. Volumnia curses them, and they attempt to leave. Virgilia says, "You shall stay too. I would I had the power / To say so to my husband" (IV, ii, 15–16). The implication is that in their relationship only Coriolanus has power; she has none, but if she had "the power," she might have kept him in Rome.

When both women are present, almost all of Coriolanus's attention and conversation is directed to his mother, and hers to him. Because Coriolanus's world is a military one, he is most comfortable when talking with his mother about war. Yet her imagery when speaking with him often deals with domestic matters, like "the ripest mulberry/That will not hold the handling" (III, ii, 79–80). She uses the image of a child wearing out its clothing to refer to his failure at winning popular approval for political office: "I would have had you put your power well on / Before you had worn it out" (III, ii, 17–18).

In the domestic third scene in the first act, a woman neighbor, Valeria, brings news of the war to Volumnia and Virgilia at their home. Learning that Coriolanus's little son, playing with a butterfly, angrily tore it to pieces, the child's mother and grandmother excuse the action as "One on's[i] father's moods." Their response suggests that they are repeating with this child the same indulgence that led to Coriolanus's adult lack of restraint.

No one (certainly not Coriolanus) enjoys more than does his mother his triumphal parade on return from Corioli and the Volscian defeat. She already has planned his next career move, into politics, as a Consul in the Roman Senate. To be granted such an office, the candidate must appeal to the citizens and demonstrate his service to Rome as measured in battle wounds. As they await his triumphal entry, Volumnia and friend Menenius count up the wounds Coriolanus has received and are delighted at the total—twenty-seven—although Virgilia shrinks from the mention of his wounds: "O no, no, no." Volumnia, in contrast, remarks: "O he is wounded, I thank the gods for't" (II, i, 119-20). That the female population of Rome regard Coriolanus as a star and a sex symbol is apparent from the grudging description of his triumphal entry by one of his enemies, the people's hypocritical tribune Brutus. He disparages the women citizens, who dress up and rush to view the "graceful posture" of Coriolanus:

*Your prattling nurse,*
*Into a rapture lets her baby cry,*
*While she chats him. The kitchen malkin*[ii]*pins*
*Her richest lockram*[iii]*'bout her reechy*[iv] *neck,*
*Clamb'ring the walls to eye him. . . . Our veiled dames*
*Commit the war of white and damask in*
*Their nicely gawded cheeks to th'wanton spoil*
*Of Phoebus' burning kisses. Such a pother,*
*As if that whatsoever god who leads him*

[i] of his [ii] maid [iii] fabric [iv] dirty

*Were slily crept into his human powers,*
*And gave him graceful posture.* (II, i, 204–19)

Unlike Coriolanus, who can hardly bear to hear accounts of his battle exploits, Volumnia revels in describing his heroism. Just before he enters with the soldiers on parade and the trumpets sounding, she heralds him as near-divine:

*Before him he carries noise, and behind him he leaves tears:*
*Death, that dark spirit, in's nervy arm doth lie,*
*Which being advanced, declines, and then men die.* (II, i, 157-60)

Coriolanus's words as he enters amid the cheering are: "No more of this, it does offend my heart." His first action, in the midst of the triumphal celebration, is to kneel before his mother for her blessing, a tradition revered in Elizabethan England. While his wife stands by, not speaking but weeping for joy, Volumnia has to call his attention to Virgilia, whom he greets as "my gracious silence" with details she would rather not hear about—the women whose husbands and children the Romans have slaughtered in Corioli. Volumnia expresses her delight not so much in Coriolanus's achievements, but in the vicarious pleasure they give her:

*I have lived*
*To see inherited*[i] *my very wishes,*
*And the buildings of my fancy. Only*
*There's one thing wanting,*[ii]*which I doubt not but*
*Our Rome will cast upon thee.* (II, i, 196-200)

She refers to the office of Consul, which she wishes Coriolanus to stand for, even though his reply (which she ignores) suggests that he does not wish to be a politician:

*Know, good mother,*
*I had rather be their servant in my way,*
*Than sway*[iii]*with them in theirs.* (II, i, 200-202)

In dealing with the citizens, he must play a part, Volumnia says, and like a stage director, she demonstrates both the action and the speech he should use:

*Go to them with this bonnet in thy hand,*
*And thus far having stretched it—here be with them,*
*Thy knee bussing*[iv] *the stones—for in such business*

[i] realized [ii] lacking [iii] rule [iv] kissing

*Action is eloquence, and the eyes of th' ignorant*
*More learn'ed than the ears—waving thy head,*
*With often thus correcting thy stout heart . . .*
*say to them*
*Thou art their soldier.* (III, ii, 73–81)

But recognizing the dishonor and degradation of acting a part alien to his nature, Coriolanus finally declares, "I will not do't."

Volumnia: *At thy choice, then. . . .*
*Do as thou list.*
*Thy valiantness was mine, thou suck'dst it from me,*
*But owe thy pride thyself.*
Coriolanus: *Pray be content.*
*Mother, I am going to the market-place:*
*Chide me no more.* (III, ii, 120–32)

In the scene in which the banished Coriolanus parts from his wife and mother, Shakespeare's source, Plutarch, reports that his mother and wife were weeping and shrieking, but this would hardly be characteristic of Shakespeare's Volumnia. As Virgilia stands by weeping and praying, Coriolanus and his mother share a tender farewell in which new feelings rise to the surface on the part of both characters. A really young Coriolanus makes the change convincing (Toby Stephens was in his twenties in the Royal Shakespeare Company production) because his arrogance and petulance can be attributed to his being both spoiled by his mother and inexperienced in all but war. He is capable of change, as this scene demonstrates.

Now he thinks of his mother, his wife, and his friends rather than of himself, and he consoles their grief. (To Volumnia) "Nay mother, / Where is your ancient courage? You were us'd / To say, extremities was the trier of spirits" (IV, i, 2–4). He quotes her again and reminds her to: "Resume that spirit when you were wont to say / If you had been the wife of Hercules, / Six of his labors you'd have done, and saved / Your husband so much sweat" (16–19). After bidding goodbye to "sweet wife," "dearest mother," and friend Cominius, he returns again to his mother: "My mother, you wot[i] well / My hazards still have been your

[i] know

solace" (27–28). Her concern now is not that he return victorious, as in sending him to war, but that he take care of himself: "Wither will thou go? Take good Cominius / With thee awhile: determine on some course / More than a wild exposure to each chance / That starts i'th'way before thee" (34–37). Cominius volunteers, but Coriolanus refuses his offer: the old man is "too full / Of the wars' surfeits to go rove with one / That's yet unbruised" (45–47). These feelings of compassion for others, new to Coriolanus, foreshadow his response to the meeting with his wife, mother, and son in the camp of the Volsces, where he goes to join their invasion of the Rome that banished him.

The final and fatal scene between Coriolanus and his family closely follows Shakespeare's source in North's Plutarch, even to having Coriolanus seated in a chair of state. Volumnia's talents at persuasion are tested to the full, but what finally convinces Coriolanus to change his determination for revenge on Rome is what the Elizabethans would call his "nature." Hidden beneath his soldier's armor, the nature that all humans share had not been allowed to reveal itself until now. His love for his family makes him accede to their wishes; he arranges a compromise between the Romans and the Volsces, their enemies whom he has joined as co-general with Aufidius.

At first, as the women and child approach him, he attempts to steel himself against his "natural" inclinations of love toward them: "All bond and privilege of nature break; / Let it be virtuous to be obstinate" (V, iii, 25–26). He vows to disassociate himself from his family: "I'll never / Be such a gosling to obey instinct[i]: but stand / As if a man were author of himself, / And knew no other kin" (34–37). His greeting to Virgilia, only his second speech to her in the play, asks forgiveness for his former behavior ("tyranny") but warns this does not include forgiveness for Rome, which has banished him. "Best of my flesh" refers to man and wife being "one flesh" (as Hamlet says), and finally he shows his affection by a kiss and vows that he has been faithful to her since they parted:

*Best of my flesh,*
*Forgive my tyranny; but do not say*
*For that, 'Forgive our Romans.' O, a kiss*

[i] natural inclination

*Long as my exile, sweet as my revenge.*
*Now, by the jealous queen of heaven, that kiss*
*I carried from thee, dear, and my true lip*
*Hath virgined it e'er since.* (V, iii, 42–48)

As is customary between parent and child, he kneels to Volumnia for her blessing, which she gives, and then in a reversal of what is "natural," she kneels to him, a move that would shock the Elizabethan audience. He denies their petition before they ask. But Volumnia's persuasive speech, which runs twenty lines for the first part and another fifty lines to its conclusion, is too much for him, and he relents.

The nobles of Rome also have petitioned Coriolanus and failed. What does Volumnia say that brings success? How does her oration have the desired effect when others have failed? First she speaks of the women's divided loyalty: How can she and Virgilia pray for his success when it means the destruction of their city? She suggests a way out, to "show a noble grace" to both sides:

*If I cannot persuade thee,*
*Rather to show a noble grace to both parts,*
*Than seek the end of one, thou shalt no sooner*
*March to assault thy country than to tread—*
*Trust to't, thou shalt not—on thy mother's womb*
*That brought thee to this world.*
Virgilia: *Ay, and mine,*
*That brought you forth this boy to keep your name*
*Living to time.* (V, iii, 120–27)

To "tread . . . on thy mother's womb" is another inversion image, bringing together the world of nurturance and that of destruction, a vivid suggestion of a "breach in nature." Coriolanus rises to leave them, but Volumnia continues. She urges him to "reconcile" the two warring sides:

*while the Volsces*
*May say 'This mercy we have showed,' the Romans,*
*'This we received,' and each in either side*
*Give the all-hail to thee, and cry 'Be blest*
*For making up this peace.'* (V, iii, 136–40)

Reconciliation is a woman's solution to the male violence and destruction of war to which she earlier committed her son. Now she casts him in a new role—that of peacemaker. Coriolanus does not reply—and then he turns away. Mother, wife, and son kneel to him and hold up their hands in supplication. He still does not answer. They rise, and Volumnia severs herself from him, the worst thing a parent can do, intensified here because of their close relationship:

*This fellow had a Volscian to his mother. . . .*
*I am hushed until our city be afire,*
*And then I'll speak a little.* (V, iii, 178–82)

Coriolanus can no longer hold out against his mother, and his gesture is more eloquent than words. The stage direction is based on North: "Holds her by the hand, silent." When he does speak, he knows that a truce will spell his doom:

*O my mother, mother: O!*
*You have won a happy victory to Rome.*
*But for your son—believe it: O believe it—*
*Most dangerously you have with him prevailed,*
*If not most mortal to him. But let it come.* (V, iii, 185–89)

Volumnia has achieved what she always dreamed of attaining—a victory by her for Rome. But the price will be the life of her son.

Aufidius, jealous of the honors his men have been paying to Coriolanus, now charges him with betrayal and calls Coriolanus a "boy of tears" who gave up "for certain drops of salt" the Volscians' conquest of Rome; "at his nurse's tears / He whined and roared away your victory" (vi, 93–98). It is the bitterest of ironies that just as Coriolanus has finally learned that achieving a peaceful coexistence can be as honorable as destroying the enemy, it is too late. The Volscian conspirators insist he must die, and the people take up the cry. Surrounded by Aufidius and his band of conspirators and denied the single combat by which he has always defeated the Volscian leader, Coriolanus is murdered by those whose violence he had been taught by his mother to admire.

## *Hamlet*—Gertrude

In *Hamlet*, Gertrude is a wife whose heart is "cleft in twain." She is in a triangular conflict that defies solution: She loves both her son, Hamlet, and her second husband, Claudius, who hate each other. As Hamlet is the central figure in Shakespeare's play, Gertrude's role should be considered not only as the king's wife who marries his murderer, as in the thirteenth-century Hamlet legend, but also as a mother. Her plight is not too unlike that of any woman who remarries, to the horror of a teenage (and Hamlet *is* such) son who idolized his own father and finds disgusting his mother's sexual relations with her new husband. To the son, she is too old for such goings-on. This attitude alone should mark him as a teenager, not as a thirty-year-old, whose reaction, especially in Elizabethan times, would be more mature.

To understand Gertrude's conflict as wife and mother, first the air must be cleared as to Hamlet's age. If he is a teenager, as I believe, it is characteristic to be upset by her remarriage and revolted by its sexual implications. There is sufficient evidence for a teenage Hamlet, who in Shakespeare's day would be considered "young," the adjective describing him throughout the play; to be thirty was to be middle-aged. Shakespeare was married with three children at twenty and died at fifty-two, an ill old man. Hamlet is attending the University of Wittenberg; young men went to university at around age fourteen, some as young as twelve. He could hardly be a university student at the age of thirty (this is Shakespeare, not Chekhov). Hamlet's youth also means that he would not confide in his mother, but rather in his peer and schoolmate, Horatio. Hamlet behaves like an angry adolescent with Gertrude. In their first scene together he is insolent, repeating her kindly meant word *seems* and flinging it back at her. As the action develops, he can misinterpret her actions, and he can "speak daggers to her"; he can plead with her to abstain from sexual relations with Claudius, but mother and son never have a rational conversation or a quiet moment together.

Where did the idea originate that Hamlet is thirty? One quarto has his age (in the graveyard scene, act V) as "xxx," with possibly an enthusiastic typesetter adding that third "x." The folio version states, regarding the gravedigger's coming to his job the day "young Hamlet" was born, "I have been sixeteene here." As actor Richard Burbage, who created the part on stage (as well as the mature roles of Macbeth, Othello, and King Lear), was well into his thirties when he played Hamlet, and if thirty is a correct reading, Shakespeare may have upped the age to accommodate his star, a practice not uncommon in today's theater.[3] Shakespeare's own son, Hamnet, who died as a child, would have been a teenager when this play was written. If Hamlet is regarded as a gifted sixteen-year-old, his revulsion at his mother's remarriage is understandable, without help from Freud or Ernest Jones. And a young Hamlet indicates a youthful Gertrude. Although as his mother, she will seem old to Hamlet ("at your age / The heyday in the blood is tame" [III, iv, 69–70]), Gertrude is in her prime and entitled to remarry.

In addition to the jealousy and disgust a remarriage might cause a youth, Hamlet receives from the ghost two more shocks about the sexual relationship between Gertrude and Claudius. First, they were having an "adulterate" relationship while she was still married to Hamlet senior; second, Claudius killed the elder Hamlet. The ghost's veracity is proved by the play within the play. "Adulterate" (I, v, 42) means what it says, that is, in an adulterous relationship.

After being rude to the new king and barely civil to Gertrude in his first appearance, Hamlet explains his behavior in a soliloquy and also offers some needed exposition. "Within a month" of the death of his father, a good and considerate man, his mother married his father's brother, jumping into bed with "wicked speed." Marriage to a deceased husband's brother was deemed "incestuous" and was forbidden by both the Protestant and the Catholic churches. What he regards as a betrayal of his beloved father by his mother colors all of Hamlet's interactions with Gertrude and comes to a climax in the scene in her "closet" or apartment in act three, evidently the first time Hamlet and his mother have been alone together since her remarriage. His sense of betrayal by both Gertrude and Ophelia, based on their hurtful actions, causes him to attack not only Ophelia but all womankind when she returns his gifts (III, i).

As mother and wife, Gertrude reacts rather than acts. The soul of patience with her son, like other mothers, she makes excuses for his rude actions and attempts to smooth over relations between him and his stepfather. In the opening scene, when Hamlet does not even reply to Claudius's thirty-line speech supposedly showing concern for his stepson, Gertrude intercedes with, "Let not thy mother lose her prayers Hamlet, / I prithee stay with us, go not to Wittenberg," that is, the university at Wittenberg (I, ii, 118–19). Still ignoring Claudius, Hamlet replies, "I shall in all my best obey you madam" (120). It is clear that Gertrude not only loves Hamlet, although she is puzzled by his actions, but that she also loves Claudius. It is obvious too that Hamlet senior was concerned for her welfare, both from Hamlet's report ("he might not beteem[i] the winds of heaven / Visit her face too roughly" I, ii, 141–42) and from the ghost's own words and actions. Concerned for her even after his death, the ghost cautions Hamlet not to harm her ("Nor let thy soul contrive / Against thy mother aught" [I, v, 85–86]) and intervenes to protect her in the closet scene when Hamlet is wildly berating her. The ghost attributes the adulterate relationship between Gertrude and Claudius to "witchcraft of his wit" and gifts that won her. A queen may have no need for gifts, but the wit may have been irresistible, especially with Hamlet senior (the older, perhaps quite a bit older, brother) away on the battlefield.

With the men doing all of the talking, Gertrude has very little to say, except for her long account of Ophelia's death. This passage of close description of a disaster by a bystander who offers no help is a literary convention dating from the ancient Greek drama. Throughout the play, Gertrude is depicted as a caring person, concerned for both her son and her husband as well as for Ophelia. As would any mother, she worries about Hamlet's future, including the prospect of marriage. Unlike Polonius, who insists to Ophelia that Hamlet is out of her "sphere," the queen says at Ophelia's grave, "I hoped thou shouldst have been my Hamlet's wife" (V, i, 237). She is puzzled by the "antic disposition" Hamlet has "put on," but she tells the more suspicious Claudius that Hamlet's behavior is caused by "His father's death, and our o'erhasty marriage" (II, ii, 57). The ghost specifically informs Hamlet that the revenge applies only to Claudius, who has committed murder, and that Gertrude is to

[i] allow

be left to heaven and her own conscience (I, v, 87–88). This means that she is not implicated in the murder, about which she knew nothing; her sins are of the flesh—adultery as well as incest, marriage to the brother of one's dead husband.

The longest scene between Hamlet and his mother takes place in act three, scene four. Beforehand, Polonius directs her to scold Hamlet, to "be round[i] with him" for upsetting Claudius by the play. In what is called "the closet scene," Hamlet is summoned to her apartment. Gertrude clearly does not know what Hamlet is referring to when he tries to implicate her in the murder of his father, and she can only repeat the first phrase as a question when he charges: "As kill as king, and marry with his brother" (III, iv, 30). Polonius, who eavesdrops once too often, is killed through the arras behind which he hides, Hamlet mistaking him for the king. Gertrude clearly is not up to the chastisement she had intended to deliver, and Hamlet takes the lead in this meeting. He accuses her, describing the sexual aspects of her marriage in terms so crude and ugly that they frighten Gertrude. As she pleads with him to stop, Hamlet succeeds in making her feel guilty:

*O Hamlet speak no more,*
*Thou turn'st mine eyes into my very soul,*
*And there I see such black and grain'ed*[ii]*spots*
*As will not leave their tinct.*[iii] (III, iv, 88–91)

Ignoring her plea to "speak no more," Hamlet attacks her relationship with Claudius for another hundred lines, even though he has long since accomplished the ghost's charge to "step between her and her fighting soul" (113). When she laments, "O Hamlet thou hast cleft my heart in twain," his stern reply is "throw away the worser part of it . . . go not to my uncle's bed" (158-61). Whether or not she will accept his advice and abstain from sex is not known. Janet Adelman notes that "for the ghost, as for Hamlet, her chief crime is her uncontrolled sexuality. But the Gertrude we see is not quite the Gertrude they see . . . we see a woman more muddled than actively wicked; even her famous sensuality is less apparent than her conflicted solicitude both for her new husband and her son."[4]

[i] forthright [ii] ingrained [iii] give up their color

Gertrude does agree to protect her son (as no doubt she would have done anyway) by not divulging that his madness is assumed. She has occasion to do just this, by replying to Claudius's query "How does Hamlet?": "Mad as the sea and wind when both contend / Which is the mightier" (IV, i, 6–8). Informing Claudius that Hamlet has "in his brainish[i] apprehension" killed Polonius, Gertrude attributes the killing to Hamlet's being mad, although she knows he was sane when he asked, hoping it was Claudius he stabbed through the arras, "Is it the king?" (III, iv, 26).

While Gertrude is shielding Hamlet, Claudius does not reveal to her his plans to send Hamlet to England with a letter ordering his death on arrival. Keenly aware of her love for her son, Claudius later explains to Laertes that in Denmark he could not appropriately punish Hamlet for Polonius's death because of the love of the people for Hamlet and also because of Gertrude's love for her son: "The Queen his mother / Lives almost by his looks" (IV, vii, 11–12). That Claudius loves Gertrude he confesses in the next lines:

*She's so conjunctive to my life and soul,*
*That as the star moves not but in his sphere,*
*I could not but by her.* (IV, vii, 14–16)

After Horatio describes Ophelia's madness, Gertrude has an aside of four lines revealing her guilt and suffering:

*To my sick soul, as sin's true nature is,*
*Each toy[ii] seems prologue to some great amiss,*
*So full of artless jealousy is guilt,*
*It spills itself, in fearing to be spilt.* (IV, v, 17–20)

Gertrude, then, is a passive, loving mother and wife who suffers guilt for her sins of the flesh. She responds to the actions of others and initiates a single action, perhaps one that is designed to save Hamlet's life by sacrificing her own. She drinks the poison cup that Claudius has prepared for Hamlet. Her physical contact with her son during the fencing match is maternal and endearing—she wipes his sweating ("fat") brow. Nothing in the text indicates whether she knows the cup is poisoned, but Claudius's "Gertrude, do not drink" is the first

[i] brainsick [ii] triviality

command of his that she does not obey, and it may be that she then realizes that the cup—meant for Hamlet, as the king said—is poisoned. She tells the king, "I will my lord, I pray you pardon me." Responding to Gertrude, which may be simultaneous with her remark to the king, Hamlet says, "I dare not drink yet madam." As Gertrude in the Laurence Olivier film, Eileen Herlie in close-up realizes the cup is poisoned as soon as Claudius drops the pearl into it, and she drinks it deliberately to save Hamlet, whose response to her is omitted. In the BBC television production, Claire Bloom's Gertrude is unaware of the poison and presents the cup to Hamlet, evoking his response.

Falling, with her dying breath, Gertrude's thoughts are for her son. She warns Hamlet against the poisoned cup and expresses her love for him. When the king says coolly, "She swoons to see them bleed," she calls out as she dies: "No, no, the drink, the drink. O my dear Hamlet, / The drink, the drink, I am poisoned" (V, ii, 314-16).

Having stabbed Claudius with the envenomed sword, Hamlet now takes up the poisoned cup and forces its contents down Claudius's throat, with an appropriate epitaph:

*Here, thou incestuous, murd'rous, damn'ed Dane,*
*Drink off this potion: Is thy union*[i] *here?*
*Follow my mother.* (V, ii, 330-32)

His farewell to his mother at last recognizes her suffering: "Wretched Queen, adieu!" (338).

## *Othello*—Desdemona and Emilia

In *Othello* the unfounded charge of infidelity against a wife is no longer a topic for farce, as in *The Merry Wives*, or romance, as in *The Winter's Tale*, but for tragedy. The other major tragedies such as *Hamlet*, *Macbeth*, and *King Lear* involve matters of national significance; *Othello* centers on marriage. The small cast, intimate setting, significance of a trivial object such as a handkerchief, and tragic consequences of marital relations gone awry characterize *Othello* as a domestic tragedy. In Shakespeare's day it was a genre increasing in popularity, demonstrated by

[i] (a) the pearl (b) union in death with Gertrude

such plays as *A Woman Killed with Kindness* and *Arden of Faversham.*

Othello's perception of his marriage to Desdemona is evident in his final speech, where he says he loved her "not wisely, but too well." Perhaps he should have said "not wisely and not well enough." The truth is that aside from their mutual physical passion, they seem to know very little about each other. Othello in his speech to the Senate declares that: "She loved me for the dangers I had passed / And I loved her that she did pity them" (I, iii, 167–68).

According to his testimony, Desdemona fell in love with Othello as an adventure hero starring in battles and sieges in exotic lands. As he recounts his exploits on visits to her father, she listens whenever she can, hastily finishing the "house affairs" to which she tends. He loved her, he says, because of her pity for the dangers he confronted. Such narrow appreciation can hardly form the basis for mutual understanding and a happy union. His glamorous presence stirs her as no suitor has among the "wealthy curled darlings" of Venice, and she takes the initiative; as Othello reports it, she would "with a greedy ear / Devour up my discourse" (149–50). "Greedy" and "devour" suggest excessive desire on her part; Hamlet uses the same metaphor to describe his mother's hanging on his father "as if increase of appetite[i] / Had grown by what it fed on" (I, ii, 144–45). Othello seems to see her as a stereotypical woman taken up with "house affairs" and hero worship.

Desdemona initiates the relationship not only by her "prayer of earnest heart" that he repeat for her ears only the entire story of his adventures but by declaring her love: "She wished that heaven had made[ii] her such a man" and that if he had a friend who loved her, he should tell her Othello's story "and that would woo her" (163–66). Othello cannot resist such a frank invitation.

Her first appearance in the play confirms his report. In front of the full Senate, gathered to appoint Othello as leader of their forces against the Turks, she holds her ground. As R. B. Heilman notes, "she has the self-possession of one whose new commitment, however romantic in origin, has enough depth to make for strength and security."[5] Responding to her father, she

[i] sexual appetite [ii] made for

announces that her former duty to him is now due to her husband and cleverly reminds Brabantio that the same was true when he married her mother. Othello's "visage," of which her father complains, is less important to her than his mind, she says, adding: "And to his honours, and his valiant parts[i] / Did I my soul and fortunes consecrate" (253–54).

His reputation and valor as a hero move her to dedicate her soul and her destiny to him, and there is innuendo in the word "parts" as parts of the body. Even more outspoken and frank are the sexual implications, if somewhat surprising to Othello, in her request to the Senate to be allowed to accompany him to Cyprus. If she is left in Venice, she says,

> *The rites[ii] for which I love him are bereft me,*
> *And I a heavy interim shall support*
> *By his dear[iii] absence.* (257-59)

"Heavy" and "support" metaphorically suggest supporting the weight of a man in sexual intercourse, an allusion also used by Cleopatra, who envies Antony's horse: "O happy horse, to bear the weight of Anthony!" (I, v, 22). After her frank request, Othello is quick to assure the Senate that he will not "scant" the "serious and great business" of warfare because of Desdemona's presence. Heilman sees this as a "self-protective" move on the part of Othello, in whose love "an over-explicit temperateness reveals some incompleteness of response . . . in which the man of affairs . . . has withheld the self from a transforming devotion."[6] From his first appearance, when Othello stresses to Iago his high-born lineage, to his last speech, reminding the state of his "service," Othello is concerned with his image, the impression he makes on others. His reaction in assuring the Senate that he will not scant their business and his quick acceptance of their request to depart immediately for Cyprus reflect this concern with self-image in a land where he is regarded as an exotic adventurer.

In Venice Othello is a highly competent hired gun who after nine months of inactivity spent in town recounting his exploits is made general of the Venetian forces in their war against the Turks. The appointment coincides with the couple's hasty elopement, the interruption of their wedding night by the call to

[i] parts of the body (double entendre) [ii] that is, of the marriage bed [iii] (a) literal (b) dire

duty, and their immediate move to Cyprus, leaving Othello and Desdemona no time together to begin developing a stable relationship. They meet, part, meet again in Cyprus, and experience a second delay of consummation caused by Cassio's drunken rioting. Because Othello's knowledge and appreciation of Desdemona as a person is so limited by time and circumstance, it is not beyond belief that he accepts the lies "honest" Iago tells him about his countrywoman: "I know our country disposition well; / In Venice they do let God see the pranks / They dare not show their husbands" (III, iii, 205–207).

Peter Erickson observes that Othello casts Desdemona in the stereotypical "cherishing maternal role and himself in the subordinate position of near-total dependence on her nurturant power."[7] In the nurturing role Desdemona adopts, she relates the small, everyday details of her caring for his welfare:

*'Tis as I should entreat you wear your gloves:*
*Or feed on nourishing dishes, or keep you warm,*
*Or sue to you to do a peculiar*[i] *profit*
*To your own person.* (III, iii, 78–81)

It is her nurturing that causes Desdemona to lose her handkerchief on which the action turns. When Othello complains of a pain on his forehead, he is thinking of the proverbial horns that grew on the brows of cuckolds, husbands of unfaithful wives. Her interpretation of the "pain" is physical, a headache:

*Faith, that's with watching,*[ii] *'twill away again;*
*Let me but bind your head, within this hour*
*It will be well again.* (289-91)

But he angrily brushes away the handkerchief she tries to apply to his head, and it falls. In Sam Mendes's 1997 production at the Royal National Theatre in London, intermission occurred at this point, and the handkerchief, spotlit, remained on the open stage to accentuate its importance. Perhaps it is not so much a dependence on Desdemona's "nurturing powers" as on preserving his self-image that convinces Othello that by her betrayal he loses everything, his "occupation's gone" (III, iii, 363).

[i] private [ii] staying awake

So far in the action, Desdemona has shown herself to be self-determined in courtship and elopement, passionate where Othello is concerned, witty in the exchange with Iago who denigrates women in his rhyming in act two, scene one, and frank in her appeal to the Senate to accompany Othello to Cyprus. Although Othello's mind is being poisoned by Iago's lies about her, she can still defend herself, and answers with spirit when Othello suggests that her hot, moist palm denotes lasciviousness:

Othello: *For here's a young and sweating devil here,*
*That commonly rebels: 'tis a good hand,*
*A frank*[i] *one.*
Desdemona: *You may indeed say so,*
*For 'twas that hand that gave away my heart.* (III, iv, 38–41)

But after Othello ascribes supernatural power to the handkerchief she has lost, Desdemona changes, almost as if she accepts the dire prophecy and is powerless to defend against it. Her loss of the handkerchief, he says, is a "fault." Passed down from woman to woman to Othello's mother, it had the power to

*make her amiable,*[ii] *and subdue my father*
*Entirely to her love: but if she lost it,*
*Or made a gift of it, my father's eye*
*Should hold her loathly*. (57–60)

"There's magic in the web of it," having been woven by a prophetic sybil, from silk spun by hallowed silkworms, and dyed in a conserve of mummified "maidens' hearts"(67–73). "The derivation of the handkerchief, from the sybil who has prophetic powers and the Egyptian charmer who 'could almost read / The thoughts of people,' (55–56) place the source of its power in women's intuitive knowledge. This knowledge enables them to use and control sexuality." When the handkerchief is lost, "the female power it symbolizes evaporates," notes Carol Thomas Neely.[8] As Othello angrily bellows for "the handkerchief," Desdemona loses her earlier self-control and resorts to lies. Next, she experiences being held "loathly," as Othello becomes violent toward her.

[i] liberal [ii] desirable

In act four, scene one, when the deputation headed by Lodovico arrive from Venice, the maddened Othello strikes her when she innocently mentions Cassio, insults her—"She can turn, and turn"[i]—and then orders her out. She goes without protest. He treats her even worse in the next scene, pretending he is in a brothel and she is a whore to whom he throws money. Twice she tries to defend herself from his accusations, but by this time she is dazed by his actions; when Emilia asks how she fares, Desdemona replies, "Faith, half asleep." She doesn't know whom Emilia is referring to by "my lord" and says, "Do not talk to me Emilia, / I cannot weep, nor answer have I none" (99–105).

Ill prepared for her former hero's abusing and insulting her, Desdemona—having made every other excuse for him, like blaming the letter calling him back to Venice—must conclude that the handkerchief's prophecy is correct: He has come to loathe her. She moves from love to fear. In the final scene, when he announces his intention to kill her, she begs for her life, but fears the worst:

*And yet I fear you, for you are fatal then,*
*When your eyes roll so: why I should fear, I know not,*
*Since guiltiness I know not, but yet I feel I fear.* (V, ii, 37–39)

Othello kills Desdemona because he fails to believe her protests that she is innocent of adultery with Cassio. Preferring to believe Iago, Othello proceeds to murder her violently. Dying, she defends him with her last breath, saying that she alone is guilty of her death, damning her soul with a lie, as Othello confesses to Emilia: "She's like a liar gone to burning hell, / 'Twas I that killed her" (130–31).

Emilia, who is not named in Shakespeare's source, appears as the wife of the ensign in Cinthio's *Hecatommithi,* where she is described as "a beautiful and honorable young woman . . . much loved by the Moor's wife and they were much together."[9] Developing the character, Shakespeare creates a woman who is loyal to Desdemona, defends her against Othello's charges when questioned, and in the intimate "willow scene" acts as a sounding board for Desdemona and as an outspoken defender of sexual freedom for women. Emilia is a supportive friend to

[i] to men

Desdemona, and their bonding contrasts with Iago's hypocritical and destructive friendship for Cassio, Roderigo, and Othello.

Emilia is first mentioned in act one, scene three in the Senate chamber when Othello instructs Iago, who is to bring Desdemona to Cyprus, "let thy wife attend on her" (296). As they await Othello's arrival in Cyprus, Emilia and Desdemona join Iago in small talk. Iago reveals himself as a misogynist in his sexual innuendo and seemingly good-natured put-downs of women. His description of Emilia as a chiding shrew evokes a response from his wife: "You ha' little cause to say so" (II, i, 108). The fact that Emilia is unaware of Iago's machinations testifies to his skill in concealing them.

Unlike the source story, in which her husband steals the handkerchief, Emilia finds it where it has dropped. She believes that Iago, who has "a hundred times / Wooed me to steal it," wants it because of the embroidery, which she will have copied ("taken out") for him:

*what he'll do with it*
*Heaven knows, not I,*
*I nothing know, but for his fantasy.*[i] (III, iii, 296–303)

She is pleased to have done something for him and announces, "I have a thing for you." But he insults her: "It is a common thing" (305–306), "thing" being slang for "vagina" and "common" implying "used by all."

As Othello grows more emotionally unstable and Desdemona more fearful, Emilia's is the one voice of reason. When questioned by Othello about Desdemona and Cassio, Emilia staunchly denies that there has been anything unlawful between them:

*I durst my lord to wager she is honest,*[ii]
*Lay down my soul at stake: if you think other,*
*Remove your thought, it doth abuse*[iii] *your bosom.* (IV, ii, 12–14)

But Othello prefers to believe Iago and dismisses Emilia as "a simple bawd," a naive go-between. She re-enters in time to hear Othello, who is treating Desdemona like a prostitute and throwing money at her, call her "that cunning whore of Venice, / That married with Othello" (91–92). When the women consult

[i] I will do it for his whim. [ii] chaste [iii] deceive

Iago about Othello's behavior, Desdemona is distraught, but Emilia shrewdly guesses the truth although she never imagines that the "rogue" could be her own husband:

*I will be hanged, if some eternal villain,*
*Some busy and insinuating rogue,*
*Some cogging, cozening*[i] *slave, to get some office,*
*Have not devised this slander.* (IV, ii, 132–35)

In scenes set in interiors suggesting a self-made enclosure, Shakespeare's women here and in *The Winter's Tale* draw closer together as if in defense against a hostile outside world. The quiet, domestic willow scene between Emilia and Desdemona takes place in Desdemona's bedroom, just before the noisy street fighting and killing. Then the action returns to the room where Desdemona will be murdered in the bed made up with her wedding sheets. Emilia is helping Desdemona undress—"Prithee unpin me" interjects Desdemona—as she recalls her mother's maid, Barbary, who "had a song of 'willow'[ii] and she died singing it" (30). Desdemona then sings the sad ballad of deserted love, ending "If I court moe women, you'll couch with moe men" (56). On the same theme, Desdemona asks Emilia whether she believes some women are unfaithful to their husbands, to which Emilia replies realistically, "There be some such, no question." "Wouldst thou do such a deed, for all the world?" asks Desdemona. Emilia: "The world is a huge thing, it is a great price, / For a small vice" (IV, iii, 63–69). When Desdemona insists, "I do not think there is any such woman," Emilia launches into a speech attacking the double standard of sexual freedom for men, and recommending equal rights for women. In its outspoken frankness, it could well have been a bombshell in its day, yet it is akin to Shakespeare's other intimate scenes between women, who discuss such subjects only among themselves. Using specific detail, Emilia progresses logically from five examples of husband's behavior that causes wives to "fall"; she then compares men and women as equal in their sexual desires and ends with three reasons why husbands "change us for others," and attributes all three reasons to women as well, justifying their behavior: if women do wrong, they have been instructed to do so by men:

[i] cheating [ii] the symbol of unrequited love

*I do think it is their husbands' faults*
*If wives do fall: say that they slack their duties*[i]
*And pour our treasures*[ii] *into foreign laps;*
*Or else break out in peevish jealousies,*
*Throwing restraint upon us: or say they strike us,*
*Or scant our former having*[iii] *in despite,*
*Why, we have galls*[iv]*: and though we have some grace,*
*Yet have we some revenge. Let husbands know,*
*Their wives have sense*[v] *like them: they see, and smell,*
*And have their palates both for sweet and sour,*[vi]
*As husbands have. What is it that they do,*
*When they change us for others? Is it sport?*[vii]
*I think it is: and doth affection*[viii] *breed it?*
*I think it doth. Is 't frailty that thus errs?*
*It is so too. And have not we affections?*
*Desires for sport? And frailty, as men have?*
*Then let them use*[ix] *us well: else let them know,*
*The ills*[x] *we do, their ills instruct us so.* (IV, iii, 86–103)

That there was objection to the passage can be seen in the fact that it is omitted in the quarto version of the play published in 1622. However, in the folio version, published in 1623 and based on the playhouse's acting script, the passage is included.

It is Emilia that Desdemona calls out to in the final scene after Othello has smothered her and to whom Desdemona lies to protect Othello; when Emilia asks, "O who has done this deed?" Desdemona, dying, says, "Nobody, I myself, farewell" (V, ii, 124–25). Only now does Emilia learn from Othello that it was Iago who instilled in Othello the belief that his wife was unfaithful to him with Cassio. Emilia cannot believe it—she has to ask four times "My husband?"—and when assured it was "thy husband, honest, honest Iago," she lashes out at Othello:

*If he say so, may his pernicious soul*
*Rot half a grain a day, he lies to th' heart,*
*She was too fond of her most filthy bargain.* (V, ii, 141–58)

In the last line Emilia expresses her view of the marriage, damaging Othello's hero image. It is she who tells Othello the

[i] sexual duties [ii] semen [iii] allowances [iv] tempers [v] sensuality [vi] that is, variety [vii] sexual enjoyment [viii] desire [ix] (a) literal (b) use sexually [x] wrongs

truth about the handkerchief, despite Iago's threatening her to keep silent:

*'Twill out, t'will: I hold my peace sir, no,*
*I'll be in speaking liberal as the air,*
*Let heaven, and men, and devils, let 'em all,*
*All, all cry shame against me, yet I'll speak.* (V, ii, 220–23)

As she continues to insist that the truth be told, Iago stabs her. Emilia dies, loyal to the last to Desdemona and intent on clearing her name. She asks to be laid with Desdemona; singing the refrain from the willow song, she drives home the truth, again detracting from Othello's heroic image with the word "cruel": "Moor, she was chaste, she loved thee cruel Moor, / So come my soul to bliss, as I speak true" (V, ii, 250–51).

Rosemary Leach as Emilia in the 1981 BBC Time-Life television production, directed by Jonathan Miller, by the clarity of her characterization effectively demonstrated Emilia's importance in the final scene. As Othello has dominated Desdemona, Emilia here assumes control over both Othello and Iago.

Throughout the action, Emilia never suspected Iago; she has accepted his put-downs and complied with his orders, like saying nothing about the handkerchief. Learning from Othello what use Iago made of the handkerchief, she now realizes her husband's perfidy and tells Othello the truth. Unlike Desdemona's pleading in vain for her life, Emilia, through her words, is able to assign the blame where it should lie—on both Iago and Othello. Complacent and accepting before, to clear Desdemona's name she now defies Iago—and he kills her for implicating him. Like Desdemona, she dies committing an unselfish act. Iago refuses to talk or reveal a motive for his actions; Othello insists on speaking.

Othello's final speech, F. R. Leavis believes, is self-dramatizing and self-justifying: he is re-creating the hero who first captured Desdemona's heart.[10] Othello claims he is "not easily jealous" (346), a claim the action has proved to be false. The murder of Desdemona, whom he states he "loved not wisely, but too well," he reduces to an exotic act; she is an object, a nonperson, a throw-away; he "Like the base Indian, threw a pearl away, / Richer than all his tribe" (348–49).

Othello at least punishes himself, stabbing himself[11] after reminding the onlookers of his service to the state as he dies. Iago, on the other hand, is described as a "dog," responsible for "the tragic loading of this bed." The final stage picture is of Emilia, Desdemona, and Othello dead upon the symbol of marriage, the bed.

In the 1995 film version, with Laurence Fishburne in the title role and Kenneth Branagh as Iago, director and adapter Oliver Parker cut the play down from a tragedy to an everyday drama of passion and violence. The role of Desdemona was so reduced that Irene Jacob could present only a one-sided character, a youthful Desdemona passionately in love with Othello. But as her witty interlude with Iago and Emilia in act two, scene one was deleted, as well as her clever response to Othello in act three, scene four (40–41), and even her defense of him with her dying breath ("Nobody, I myself"), her Desdemona has no backbone. A weakened heroine, she is merely a victim. At times, her foreign accent is intrusive. Anna Patrick fares better with Emilia, starting in a low key and in the background, she becomes more prominent until she convincingly delivers her defense of sexual freedom for women in the willow interlude and dies in the final scene accusing Othello and Iago and defending Desdemona.

*Macbeth*—Lady Macbeth

In *Macbeth,* Lady Macbeth has a dual role. Without her Macbeth would never have carried out the murder of Duncan to attain the promised crown. She sacrifices her selfhood to further Macbeth's ambition; although he first thinks of the murder, it is she who urges him on when his resolve falters. In addition, the dialogue between the pair expresses their love; on this love depends the fulfillment of Macbeth's goal, not just the crown, but "a line of kings" to succeed him and Lady Macbeth.

Images of babies and nurturing associated with Lady Macbeth reinforce Macbeth's ambition for the crown and for their children as heirs to the crown. Older critics might dismiss Lady Macbeth, as Samuel Johnson does, as "merely detested," or note, like A. C. Bradley, that "it is an error to regard her as remarkable on the intellectual side."[12] But the couple bear equal weight in this tragedy. If Macbeth's tragic flaw is his "vaulting ambition" (I, vii, 27), Lady Macbeth's is her loss of selfhood, her deliberate sublimation of her true nature to serve her husband's ambition. His obsession is directly associated with his love for his wife and his desire to create a dynasty that will represent them both. Of the available film versions, including those made by the BBC and by Orson Welles, the love relationship between Macbeth and Lady Macbeth is best demonstrated in the 1971 movie directed by Roman Polanski and adapted by Kenneth Tynan, with Jon Finch in the title role and Francesca Annis as Lady Macbeth. Ms. Annis's performance also is the best of the three versions; not only her great talent but also her youth and beauty contribute to a sympathetic portrait of a wife who assumes her husband's aims as her own and who at the end, tormented by guilt, destroys herself just as she has earlier destroyed her womanhood.

The love that exists between the pair is clearly demonstrated in the text; children will be the fruit of that love and will carry on their line. But in *Macbeth* "fair" is "foul" (Macbeth's first words in the play), good is twisted and inverted, Lady Macbeth exchanges her milk for gall, and images of infanticide invade the usual connotation of babies. In Macbeth's letter, he describes her as his "dearest partner of greatness" a phrase incorporating both his love and the "greatness" they will share as partners (I, v, 10). But as soon as she reads the letter, Lady Macbeth's first image is one of inversion. Milk, a nurturing image associated with babies, becomes a hindrance; she reflects that her husband's nature is "too full o' th' milk of human kindness / To catch the nearest way." (Both she and Goneril in *King Lear* [IV, ii, 50] disparage a man with commendable human kindness, which they associate with milk and suggest that he is less of a man. Shakespeare proves them wrong.) Realizing that this kindness is an impediment to his aim, she will force him to the cruelty that is "the nearest way" to the crown. Just as Macbeth's nature will be diverted from its course, so she must help him by divesting herself of her womanly nature of compassion. In a speech that spells her doom, she invokes evil spirits to "unsex" her, to exchange her naturally kind instincts for "direst cruelty": "Come to my woman's breasts / And take my milk for gall" (I, v, 40-48).

Her next image is another one of inversion, like nurturing milk exchanged for gall. She asks night to hide the wound she is prepared to inflict:

*That my keen knife see not the wound it makes,*
*Nor Heaven peep through the blanket of the dark,*
*To cry, 'Hold, Hold.'* (I, v, 50-54)

In the belief that the word "blanket" is a misprint or misreading of the original manuscript, editors have attempted to alter it. Coleridge suggested "blank height" as an emendation. But as a nurturing image the 1623 reading makes perfect sense. "Blanket" is a comforting allusion associated with sleep, and "heaven" suggests angels, usually represented as cherubim, like those Macbeth later refers to (I, vii, 22). To couple a murder in the previous line with this image of babies peeping over a blanket typifies the inversion of good and evil to be found throughout the play.

Macbeth's first words to Lady Macbeth, "dearest partner of greatness" and "dearest love," are indicative of the love between them. One tragic result of the ensuing action will be the destruction of that love. Because she loves him and knows him so well, Lady Macbeth is confident that she can motivate him to achieve the crown he so desperately craves. She never realizes the price she must pay, which is nothing less than her selfhood. But she is not the instigator of the murder. It is already in Macbeth's mind, as he first reveals in an aside when the witches hail him as Glamis, Cawdor, and king:

*Why do I yield to that suggestion,*[i]
*Whose horrid image doth unfix my hair*
*And make my seated heart knock at my ribs*
*Against the use of nature . . . .*
*My thought, whose murder yet is but fantastical,*[ii]
*Shakes so my single state of man . . .* (I, iii, 134–40)

Duncan's murder is an act neither would be capable of alone. They will work in concert to achieve the crown that brings with it consequences they could not foresee. After promising Macbeth that she will carry out the act herself: "You shall put / This night's great business into my dispatch" (I, v, 68), Lady Macbeth, we learn later, backs out. Once in Duncan's bedchamber, she cannot murder him because, she says, he "resembled my father as he slept" (II, ii, 11–12).

[i] temptation [ii] that is, in my mind

Macbeth attempts to retreat, too, and might have done so except for the "chiding" to which she knows he will respond. After calling him a coward twice (to no avail) she uses an allusion terrible and frightening—the murder of one's own helpless infant:

*I have given suck, and know*
*How tender 'tis to love the babe that milks me:*
*I would, while it was smiling in my face,*
*Have plucked my nipple from his boneless gums,*
*And dashed the brains out, had I so sworn*
*As you have done to this.* (I, vii, 54–59)

Inversion again intensifies the image: The last three lines shatter a picture of a loving, nursing mother. It has the desired effect: Macbeth will act, fearing only failure. He is again convinced, admires his wife's courage, and expresses a thought often in the minds of loving couples, to pass on to their children the qualities one admires in one's partner: "Bring forth men children only." But again the chord of inversion is struck; she is using the "mettle"[i] he admires to serve destruction.

Despite critics' misinterpretation, the Macbeths have had children and hope to have more, as indicated by the lines just quoted. In light of what will happen to their relationship, it is important to recognize it, as first portrayed, as a loving marriage that includes children. If evidence in Shakespeare's plays is considered as information the audience needs to know, "I have given suck" reveals that they have had at least one child, and Macbeth's response here indicates that they expect more. Children and the succession will be stressed more as the play progresses, and the images and allusions reveal the deeper motive of Macbeth's ambition, the desire not only to be king but to be first of "a line of kings." As he is to be the father, she will be the mother. Together they will found a dynasty; both are central to the succession Macbeth hopes to father.

When the witches hail Macbeth as Cawdor, Glamis, and king, Banquo asks them to "look into the seeds of Time, / And say which grains will grow" (I, iii, 59). They then hail Banquo: "Thou shalt get[ii] kings, though thou be none" (67). The witches'

[i] spirit, toughness (like metal) [ii] beget

promise that Banquo's descendants will be kings so preys on Macbeth's mind that he cannot refrain from mentioning it twice to Banquo in this scene (86, 118). Once he becomes king, Macbeth is shaken by the thought that according to the witches, no son of his will succeed him. If so, he has given his "eternal jewel"[i] to the devil, "To make them kings, the seed of Banquo kings" (III, i, 67, 69). Macbeth will challenge the prophecy.

Lady Macbeth's allusion to infanticide is preceded by another baby image spoken by Macbeth. At the beginning of scene eight in the first act, during the welcoming banquet for Duncan (another ironic twist to nurturing), Macbeth resolves not to kill so good a king, for whom all will mourn. In addition, Macbeth fears discovery of the murder by the cherubim, who were believed to be God's spies, accompanied by Pity, personified as a baby in heaven like the cherubim. Continuing the wind imagery, the babies will make known to the world the "horrid deed" by blowing it in every eye, at which all will weep in a flood of tears:

*Pity, like a naked new-born babe,*
*Striding the blast, or Heaven's cherubin, horsed*
*Upon the sightless couriers of the air,*[ii]
*Shall blow the horrid deed in every eye,*
*That tears shall drown the wind.* (I, vii, 21–25)

In 1949 Cleanth Brooks called attention to the "naked babe" as a central symbol. "It is because of his hopes for his own children and his fears of Banquo's that he [returns] to the witches," there to witness the apparitions of two babies, "the crowned babe and the bloody babe."[13] Yet Brooks failed to associate the baby images with Lady Macbeth, whom he classifies as one of Shakespeare's "villains" and claims she was ambitious, although there is no textual evidence of her being so. The baby images, together with those of nurturing, reveal not only the impetus for Macbeth's ambition but also a deeper and more human character than that with which Lady Macbeth has been credited.

The murder sequence begins with a nurturing allusion—Macbeth commanding a servant, "bid thy mistress, when my

[i] that is, his soul [ii] clouds (shaped like horses)

drink is ready / She strike upon the bell"(II, i, 31–32). Again the commonplace is inverted: The comforting drink she has prepared becomes a signal for murder. As the bell sounds and Macbeth departs, Lady Macbeth enters, alone, revealing that she has had to bolster up her courage by drinking some of the liquor she prepared and doctored for Duncan's guards: "That which hath made them drunk hath made me bold" (II, ii, 1). But as soon as Macbeth appears, altered and shaken by the murder, she is forced to revert to her "chastising" role. Even though she attacks him as "infirm of purpose," he refuses to return the bloody daggers to the scene, despite her insistence that he has nothing to fear, comparing his state to that of a child afraid of a picture:

*The sleeping and the dead,*
*Are but as pictures: 'tis the eye of childhood*
*That fears a painted devil.* (II, ii, 52–54)

She who could not harm the sleeping Duncan because he resembled her father must now force herself to confront him, dead and bleeding, to steep the daggers in his blood and place them by the grooms, and to assure Macbeth that "a little water clears us of this deed" (66). The scene in which she has acted with superb self-control will come back to haunt her when she lacks all control, walking in her sleep. When the dead king is discovered and Macbeth defends his double murder of the grooms in hyperbolic, overblown language, Lady Macbeth, who has been playing the role of concerned hostess, briefly reverts to the womanly nature she subverted: She faints.

Shakespeare departs from his source, Holinshed, which recounts that Macbeth's wife "was very ambitious, burning in unquenchable desire to bear the name of a queen."[14] Despite critics asserting that she was ambitious, there is no textual evidence for such a charge. When she reads his letter and first learns of the witches' prophecy, she says:

*Hie thee hither,*
*That I may pour my spirits in thine ear,*
*And chastise with the valor of my tongue*
*All that impedes thee from the golden round,*
*Which fate and metaphysical aid doth seem*
*To have thee crowned withal.* (I, v, 25–30)

She thinks of Macbeth, not of herself, as attaining and wearing the "golden round" of the crown, referring to him alone by using "thee" twice, not "us."

Shakespeare's Lady Macbeth never reveals even a hope to be queen. She has buried any personal hopes she may have had for the future, for these are never voiced, only her determination that he achieve his own desire for the crown. This accomplished, she enters in act three as queen, miserable and alone:

*Nought's had, all's spent,*
*Where our desire is got without content:*
*'Tis safer, to be that which we destroy,*
*Than by destruction dwell in doubtful*[i] *joy.* (III, ii, 4–7)

But as soon as Macbeth appears, she must hide her unhappiness and bend all her efforts to support him. No longer is their relationship close. Although in her earlier scenes she almost always appears with her husband, now she asks why he keeps himself "alone." Though he still addresses her in affectionate idiom like "dearest chuck" and "dear wife," her terms for him are now formal: "My Lord," at the beginning of her first two speeches to him, and "you" while he still employs the affectionate "thou," which formerly both used. Although he no longer needs her help to plan and execute the murders, he does confide to her his "fears in Banquo." She assures him in her usual vein of comforting, "But in them Nature's copy's not eterne," that is, the succession of Banquo's children need not go on eternally (38).

Macbeth's plot against Banquo and Fleance carries forward the theme of succession. Although the witches have predicted that Banquo will beget kings, Macbeth defies fate and orders Banquo and Fleance murdered. Fleance, however, escapes the murderers sent by Macbeth to waylay the two on their way to the banquet honoring the thanes, including Banquo.

This second banquet, an inverted nurturing image, will be interrupted by the appearance only to Macbeth of the gory ghost of his victim, Banquo, blood dripping from "twenty trench'ed gashes on his head." In one of his wild speeches to the ghost, Macbeth challenges him to come to life again and fight in an

[i] fearful

encounter less fearful to him: "If trembling I inhabit then, protest[i] me / The baby of a girl," that is, a baby girl (III, iv, 104). The baby reference sustains the continuing images of succession and presages the babies to appear on stage, two of them as apparitions and one, in stage practice, in the arms of Lady Macduff at the massacre of her family.

When Macbeth almost reveals the murder of Banquo to the assembled thanes, Lady Macbeth saves him. She takes charge and assumes her "chiding" role, with such asides to him as: "O proper stuff," "Fie, for shame," and "Quite unmanned in folly?" (III, iv, 59, 73, 72). First she makes excuses for him to the guests, but when they begin to ask questions, she dismisses them. The scene ends with her concern for Macbeth and his lack of sleep, "the season of all natures" (140). Although she has not changed outwardly, her troubled mind has been revealed in the brief soliloquy as queen at the beginning of act three. Macbeth, shaken and fearful, is hardly recognizable. Having lost all sense of the wrongdoing which so troubled him at the outset, he now announces:

> *I am in blood*
> *Stepped in so far, that should I wade no more,*
> *Returning were as tedious as go o'er.* (III, iv, 135–37)

The baby apparitions in Macbeth's final meeting with the witches support his constant awareness that succession is a response to the mutability of Time. When Macbeth conjures the witches to answer him, he addresses them in images opposed to creation. He invokes the destruction of the world, its buildings, its crops, its oceans, and even its seeds, synonymous with babies in symbolizing growth and hope:

> *Though the treasures*
> *Of Nature's germens*[ii] *tumble all together,*
> *Even till destruction sicken: answer me.* (IV, i, 58–60)

A parallel to Macbeth's catalog of destruction, the cauldron has been prepared by the witches with cannibalized ingredients, including "finger of birth-strangled babe / Ditch-delivered by a drab"[iii] (30–31), an inversion image of infanticide echoing Lady Macbeth's earlier allusion. When the baby apparitions appear,

[i] proclaim [ii] seeds [iii] prostitute

the bloody babe is a positive image, here contrasting to the witch's "birth-strangled" allusion. Misinterpreting the apparitions, Macbeth feels encouraged, believing the bloody babe indicates that "man of woman born" never will vanquish him. But it actually represents the birth of his nemesis, Macduff, who was not born in the usual way but "untimely ripped" from his mother's womb by Caesarean section. The baby holding a tree assures Macbeth of his safety until Birnham wood comes to his castle at Dunsinane, an event he assumes to be impossible, unaware of the strategy of camouflage. But the tree also represents the family tree of Banquo, whose line will inherit the throne. The apparition on his "baby-brow" wears a crown, and the "show of eight kings" plus many others demonstrates the succession from that crown, including the patron of Shakespeare's company, King James I, before whom *Macbeth* was performed.

The first apparition, an armed head, warns Macbeth against Macduff. Macbeth will respond by destroying not Macduff, who has fled to England, but his family. Ranking for sheer horror with the putting out of Gloucester's eyes in *King Lear* is the massacre of Lady Macduff and her children. Macbeth vows to

> *Seize upon Fife; give to th' edge o' th' sword*
> *His wife, his babes, and all unfortunate souls*
> *That trace him in his line.* (IV, i, 151–53)

Immediately after this, Lady Macduff appears on stage with her little son in an endearing domestic scene, interrupted by the appearance of Macbeth's murderers. They kill her, the boy, and, in most performances, the baby in her arms: "all my pretty chickens and their dam," grieves Macduff. When Ross delivers the sad news to him in England, young Malcolm twice tries to console him: "Give sorrow words" and "Be comforted." Almost angrily, Macduff breaks in, saying to Ross, "he has no children," referring to Malcolm and his well-meant but trite condolences[15] (IV, iii, 213–16). Although some, including Freud, believe that "he" refers to an impotent Macbeth, the text is clear that the Macbeths have had children. "I have given suck" says Lady Macbeth, and he laments that Banquo's children will be kings, "no son of mine succeeding." His "bring forth men children only" expresses a hope for males eligible to succeed to the crown.

Until the sleepwalking scene in act five, the audience has known little of the inner workings of Lady Macbeth's mind since Duncan's murder, although her despair as the new queen signals the breakdown to come. Earlier all her efforts were directed to one end—attaining the crown for Macbeth. Knowing his nature, she realized that chastisement to the point of insult would be needed to force him to act. What she could not know—what neither knew—is that once he entered that sea of blood, he would continue: "returning were as tedious as go o'er" (III, iv, 137). They combine forces to bring about the first murder, but thereafter Macbeth acts alone. Without her help or foreknowledge he murders first the two grooms, then Banquo by hired killers, and next the Macduff family and their household staff. But Lady Macbeth becomes aware of all the murders and assumes the guilt while concealing her feelings, a response she earlier recommended to Macbeth. In the second banquet scene she plays the role of a congenial hostess while supporting a distraught Macbeth. Finally, having to sublimate her natural feelings proves too much. They come to the fore when she has no control over them—when she is asleep.

At the beginning of act five, a doctor discusses her sleepwalking with "a Waiting-Gentlewoman," who reports that Lady Macbeth in "a most fast sleep" will rise from her bed, take paper from her cabinet, and will "fold it, write upon't, read it, afterwards seal it, and again return to bed." The doctor comments, "A great perturbation in nature, to receive at once the benefit of sleep, and do the effects of watching."[i] (V, i, 4-10). Some critics interpret the letter she seems to be writing as a warning to Lady Macduff or to Macbeth, "indicating that she still wishes to control him."[16]

Most likely she is reenacting the writing and reading of Macbeth's letter that she is holding in her initial appearance, the letter that is the first link in the chain of events leading to the murder of Duncan. As she sleepwalks, she reenacts that murder and confuses it with later ones. For all, she suffers guilt symbolized by the blood she believes still stains her hands, which she continually washes.

[i] waking

Each of the details contributes to a picture of a soul in torment. The light she has commanded to be with her at all times contrasts with the blackness she invoked to conceal the murder of Duncan and in which she now finds herself: "Hell is murky." She is reliving her chastisement of Macbeth: "Fie, my lord, fie, a soldier, and afeard?" The trauma of seeing the dead Duncan is revealed in a line of chilling monosyllables: "Who would have thought the old man to have had so much blood in him." More murders crowd the reenactment as she addresses Macbeth: "The thane of Fife[i] had a wife; where is she now?" "I tell you yet again Banquo's buried; he cannot come out on's grave"(35–60). Chorus-like, the doctor and the gentlewoman comment on the action: "The heart is sorely charged," observes the doctor, who adds, "this disease is beyond my practice"(51–55). The scene concludes as did the actual episode it mirrors: Lady Macbeth tells her husband to wash his hands and put on his dressing-gown, hears the knocking at the gate, and leads him off to bed, to which she will now return: "Come, come, come, come, give me your hand: / What's done cannot be undone. To bed, to bed, to bed" (V, i, 63–65).

It is the final irony of their marriage that after their love together, hopes for their children, and suffering apart, the report of her death hardly registers with Macbeth, who comments: "She should have died hereafter," meaning "she would have died anyway" (V, v, 17). Because he has "supped full with horrors,"[17] with her death he dies spiritually, and pronounces what is possibly the most cynical of Shakespeare's passages on time and mutability, beginning "Tomorrow, and tomorrow, and tomorrow." This most pessimistic metaphor for life concludes with the word both Macbeth and Lady Macbeth used earlier to describe the state of kingship for which they sold themselves:

*It is a tale*
*Told by an idiot, full of sound and fury*
*Signifying nothing.* (V, v, 26–28)

*Macbeth* ends like the chronicle play it is in part. The highest-ranking person, who is Malcolm, delivers the final speech, restoring order to the realm and describing Macbeth and Lady

[i] Macduff

Macbeth not as they were earlier but as what they became: "this dead butcher and his fiend-like Queen"(V, ix, 35). Neither of the two principals is given a dying speech. She, we learn, is said to have committed suicide, and his head is brought in on a pole. Order returns to Scotland, not through their efforts but despite them. Nevertheless, the play is not a history but a tragedy. Its plot has been and is still being repeated in novels, dramas, and movies, not to mention real life: Two people whose love makes them inseparable act in concert to commit a murder and destroy not only the victim but their loving relationship. Macbeth goes his own frantic way, driven by "vaulting ambition" and fear, wading deeper and deeper in blood. Lady Macbeth, in a characteristically female way suffers in silence, her only concern the aims and well-being of her partner. In the end she is broken and destroyed by the burden of guilt and retribution, the existence of which she had refused to recognize.

*King Lear*—Regan and Goneril

In *King Lear*, Regan and Goneril are married women in love—but not with their husbands. Regan and Goneril are rivals for the love of Edmund, Gloucester's handsome[18] son, whose ingratitude and villainy matches their own. In the earlier versions of the Lear story they figure as ungrateful daughters in contrast to the faithful Cordelia. Shakespeare adds the Gloucester story and uses Edmund as the link between the two plots. The trio become personifications of evil, displaying all of the seven deadly sins, especially lust. As Shakespeare differentiates the evil natures of the sisters, so he contrasts their relationships with their husbands. Regan and Cornwall are two of a kind, aiding and encouraging each other as they cruelly torture Gloucester, whereas Albany recognizes his wife, Goneril, for what she is. His nature and hers are opposites.

The confrontation between Lear and Goneril ends with Lear's invoking the goddess Nature to: "Into her womb convey sterility, / Dry up in her the organs of increase" (I, iv, 276–77). Lear's outbursts on this theme, blaming procreation that produced such daughters, will continue. When Albany appears at the end of the scene with conciliatory remarks, Goneril criticizes him for his "milky gentleness" (340). Although Goneril intends this allusion as an insult, it actually marks Albany as having the commendable trait of compassion, usually associated with women, a trait he demonstrates throughout the play in contrast to Goneril's lack of womanly characteristics.

If Goneril is bad, Regan is worse; it is she who shuts the gates against Lear in the raging storm and it is she who insists to Cornwall that both Gloucester's eyes be put out. When a servant attacks and wounds Cornwall to prevent him from doing so, Regan takes Cornwall's sword and kills the servant. In the television film of Olivier's *King Lear*, Diana Rigg as Regan refuses when the dying Cornwall says "Give me your arm" (III, vii, 96), and leaving him to die on the floor, she exits, looking satisfied at the advantage she now holds in the rivalry over Edmund.

The evil sisters' lust for Edmund brings about their downfalls. Both make advances to him and he encourages both, while cynically debating whether to accept either.

*To both these sisters have I sworn my love,*
*Each jealous of the other as the stung*
*Are of the adder. Which of them shall I take?*
*Both? One? Or neither?* (V, i, 55–58)

As the British gather their armies to meet the French, who have "landed," Goneril, in a passage filled with sexual innuendo, kisses Edmund, gives him a gift (probably a chain), hints that he might "venture" to kill her husband Albany, and complains that she must "change arms at home, and give the distaff / Into my husband's hands." That is, she must take up arms in the ensuing battle because woman-like Albany is incapable as a battle leader (IV, ii, 15–24). Like so many of the sisters' statements, this is a lie, for Albany proves to be an ideal leader, winning the battle and showing compassion for defeated Lear and Cordelia. He demands they be delivered to him, but Edmund has already ordered their deaths.

Albany voices the audience's sentiments when he confronts Goneril with the sisters' inhumane treatment of their father and predicts that such bestial behavior will be self-destructive:

*It will come.*
*Humanity must perforce prey on itself,*
*Like monsters of the deep.* (IV, ii, 47–49)

Replying, Goneril again couples him with an allusion to milk—"Milk-livered man"—and concludes the conversation with a contemptuous, "Marry, your manhood—mew!" (50, 68). Although in Goneril's distorted view his manhood is as weak as a kitten, Albany is more of a complete man than the devious and villainous Edmund. As in Albany's accusation, the sisters are often compared to monsters and to beasts of prey like wolves, serpents, and tigers. In the Olivier film, with strong performances by Dorothy Tutin as Goneril, Diana Rigg as Regan, and Robert Lindsay as Edmund, the triangle is very much in the forefront of the action in the second half of the play. If these three experts in treachery and cruelty were to join forces they might prevail, but the sisters' lustful rivalry will defeat them.

Being inhuman monsters, the sisters cannot be killed by others but must self-destruct. After the battle is won, at the head of the English forces Albany enters with Goneril, and Regan appears with Edmund, who is commanding her forces, and over whom the sisters begin to quarrel. Infuriated that her widowed sister might marry Edmund, Goneril has written to him proposing that he kill Albany to clear the way for them to marry. She has poisoned her sister, who crying "sick, O sick," departs the scene, declaring Edmund her "lord and master." While Goneril gloats in an aside, Albany shows compassion, directing "She is not well, convey her to my tent," where she dies (106). Goneril's treacherous letter to Edmund is discovered; in proving Edmund a traitor, his brother, Edgar, mortally wounds him in combat. Offstage, Goneril kills herself, "a bloody knife" brought on as evidence. Albany orders the sisters' bodies to be brought in: "This judgment of the heavens that makes us tremble, / Touches us not with pity" (V, iii, 230–31).

Director Peter Brook's 1971 acclaimed black-and-white movie version of *King Lear*, with Paul Scofield in the title role should be mentioned if only in contrast to the Olivier television film. The latter is the truer and more complete interpretation, but the very starkness of the Brook movie is a compelling and appropriate setting for the tragedy. Irene Worth as Goneril and Susan Engel as Regan are presented as visual contrasts: Goneril is pure cruelty personified in her cold, etched features, while Regan seems soft and attractive, so that her villainy shocks the audience even more. Their rivalry over Edmund is truncated, as is much of the script, in favor of vast stretches of desolate landscape.

## Notes

[1] Harley Granville-Barker, *Prefaces to Shakespeare*, II, 377.

[2] Alice Griffin, *The Sources of Ten Shakespearean Plays*, 188.

[3] Alice Griffin, *Rebels and Lovers*, 296–97.

[4] Janet Adelman, *Suffocating Mothers*, 15.

[5] Robert B. Heilman, *Magic in the Web*, 173.

[6] Ibid., 174.

[7] Peter Erickson, *Patriarchal Structures in Shakespeare's Dramas*, 93.

[8] Carol Thomas Neely, "Women and Men in *Othello*," in *The Woman's Part*, ed. Carolyn Lenz, Gayle Greene, and Carol Neely, 228–29.

[9] Griffin, *Sources*, 229.

[10] F. R. Leavis, *The Common Pursuit*, 142.

[11] Laurence Olivier used a switch-blade dagger concealed in his bracelet.

[12] A. C. Bradley, *Shakespearean Tragedy*, 371.

[13] Cleanth Brooks, *The Well Wrought Urn*, 42.

[14] Griffin, *Sources*, 249.

[15] This is convincingly demonstrated by Jon Finch as Macbeth in the 1971 film directed by Roman Polanski.

[16] Kenneth Muir, ed., Arden *Macbeth*, 142, n. 6.

[17] Another inversion of a nurturing image.

[18] He invokes "Nature" as his "goddess" (I, ii, 1), suggesting he is endowed with naturally good looks.

# SECTION III.

## RELATIONSHIPS

When both Goneril and Regan develop a passion for Edmund in *King Lear*, it is as much a case of evil recognizing a soulmate as it is boredom with marriage and the sexual attraction of a young, handsome man with more spirit than either of the husbands. But in history plays other than *King Lear*, set in the early days of Britain, women who indulge in affairs or extramarital relationships are French, like Margaret in the *King Henry VI* trilogy, Trojan like Cressida, Greek like Helen, or Egyptian like Cleopatra.

In *Titus Andronicus*, Shakespeare's earliest tragedy, Roman empress Tamora, a Goth, has an affair with and a child by Aaron the Moor, whose cruelty matches her own. Beyond revenge for the deaths of her sons when Titus and his Romans defeated the Goths, there is little motivation of this character in a play filled with deception, disguises, betrayal, feigned madness, mutilation, and rape. Along with predecessors of its type, Marlowe's *The Jew of Malta* and Kyd's *The Spanish Tragedy, Titus Andronicus* was evidently popular, for it appeared in three quarto editions, the first in 1594. In the BBC Time-Life television production Eileen Atkins uses her considerable talents to humanize Tamora, but the character and the play are difficult for modern audiences to accept. Julie Taymor in her recent movie *Titus* attempts with some success to humanize the characters by casting Anthony Hopkins as Titus and Jessica Lange as Tamora. After this early attempt, Shakespeare meets the challenge of developing credible legendary heroines within the framework of their fame.

# CHAPTER EIGHT: ENGLISH AND CLASSICAL HISTORIES

*King Henry VI, Troilus and Cressida,* and *Antony and Cleopatra*

*King Henry VI*—Margaret

Margaret of Anjou becomes Queen of England and then leader of the Lancastrian troops in the Wars of the Roses, only to see her son and husband killed and her throne lost as the Yorks assume power. In the course of the Henry trilogy and *Richard III,* Margaret is a Shakespearean rarity—a character who develops from youth to old age in four plays. Though not exactly a role model, Margaret exhibits many of the traits of Shakespeare's female characters. She is strong-minded, clever, resourceful, determined, ambitious for her child, and unstoppable once embarked on a course of action. As a young woman aware of her own sensuality, she uses it to advantage to attain her goals. She also is cruel and vengeful to enemies, and she disdains forgiveness. Advanced in years in *King Richard III,* she has lost her political power and her physical strength, but she still is in command verbally and uses words as weapons.

In the *King Henry VI* trilogy Margaret is introduced in part one as a young and beautiful woman captured by the Earl of Suffolk in the English defeat of the French at Anjou. Taking a hint from historian Hall, who reports that Suffolk was "the Queen's darling," Shakespeare creates this unhistorical incident. Margaret is down-to-earth and realistic in the encounter, in contrast to Suffolk, who is smitten with love at first sight and spouting sonnet language. Margaret identifies herself as the daughter of the King of Naples and asks what ransom she is to pay, the customary practice for captured nobility. As Margaret questions him, Suffolk in asides debates how he, a married man, may "win this Lady Margaret. For whom? / Why for my king" (V, iii, 88–89). Margaret, in her asides, first believes he may be mad, but then decides practically she may as well see where the conversation will lead: "He seems a knight / And will not any way dishonor me" (101–102). Suffolk asks whether she would consider "Your bondage happy,[i] to be made a queen?" Margaret's reply is a cleverly worded request to be set free:

*To be a queen in bondage is more vile,*
*Than is a slave in base servility:*
*For princes should be free.* (111–14)

By now, she is aware of her effect on Suffolk, who elaborates: "I'll undertake to make thee Henry's queen. . . . If thou will condescend to be my—" Margaret: "What?" Suffolk: "His love." The intentional slip is not lost on Margaret, who consents, if it "please" her father. Margaret's father agrees, on the condition that he be granted the French regions of Maine and Anjou, to which amorous Suffolk readily agrees, giving away lands hard won by the English. Margaret is all maiden modesty as she replies to Suffolk's request for a message he may deliver to King Henry: "Such commendations as becomes a maid, / A virgin, and his servant, say to him" (177–78). Suffolk persists, asking for a kiss for Henry, and kissing her. Margaret's delicate reply is a signal to Suffolk that her emotions respond to his: "That for thyself: I will not so presume / To send such peevish tokens to a king" (185–86).

From that instant on, their mutual infatuation will not bode well for the reigning Lancasters. Suffolk's "wondrous rare description" of her persuades King Henry to marry such a paragon of beauty and virtue, although he is already engaged to another lady, a liaison supported by the Duke of Gloucester and the court. Margaret will enter her reign with powerful enemies.

With the English lords in dissension over the marriage, *King Henry VI* part two opens with Margaret as queen, having undergone a marriage ceremony in France with Suffolk as the king's deputy. On her arrival at Henry's court, Margaret's

[i] fortunate

modest speech to the king belies her affair with Suffolk, by then well under way. Henry thanks the Lord for blessing him with Margaret and hopes that "sympathy of love unite our thoughts." Margaret assures him she has shared that thought "By day, by night, waking, and in my dreams, / In courtly company, or at my beads" (I, i, 23–27). Henry is as ecstatic as Suffolk was:

*Her sight did ravish, but her grace in speech,*
*Her words y-clad with wisdom's majesty,*
*Makes me from wond'ring fall to weeping joys.* (I, i, 32–34)

Only two scenes later, her tone and actions change drastically as she complains to Suffolk about the proud behavior of the Duke of Gloucester, the Lord Protector:

*What, shall King Henry be a pupil still,*
*Under the surly Gloucester's governance?*
*Am I a queen in title and in style,*
*And must be made a subject to a duke?* (I, iii, 47–49)

Her speech has changed along with her demeanor, from clever hesitancy to "words y-clad with wisdom's majesty" to taunting questions denigrating her husband. Margaret will soon move from verbal to physical attacks.

As Henry is a saintly king who wishes he had been born a shepherd, Margaret becomes stronger as he grows weaker and more indecisive. After warning Henry, "the welfare of us all / Hangs on the cutting short that fraudful man" (II, iii, 81), she and Suffolk have Gloucester arrested and then murdered in his bed. Suffolk is suspected, but Margaret defends him to Henry in a forty-line speech shifting attention to herself as a neglected and suffering wife: "Is all thy comfort shut in Gloucester's tomb? / Why then Dame Margaret was n'er thy joy" (III, ii, 78–79). She reminds him of the troublesome voyage and heavy winds encountered when she came from France to marry Henry, a sign that should have warned her to "set no footing on this unkind shore":

*The pretty vaulting sea refused to drown me,*
*Knowing that thou wouldst have me drowned on shore*
*With tears as salt as sea, through thy unkindness.* (III, ii, 94–96)

Despite her defense of Suffolk, the king rightly accuses him of Gloucester's death and banishes him. When Margaret and Suffolk part, it is evident that her affair has lost none of its ardor:

*Even thus two friends condemned*
*Embrace and kiss, and take ten thousand leaves,*
*Loather a hundred times to part than die.* (III, ii, 353–55)

But Suffolk is not only banished; he is put to death and his head is sent to Margaret. A far cry from the sensitive soul she has pretended to be and presaging her behavior on the battlefield, she fondles the head.

In the Wars of the Roses between the houses of York and Lancaster, King Henry is frozen with fear when the Yorks are winning. His weakness dictates that Margaret assume leadership of the Lancastrian forces as she orders retreat:

Queen: *Away, my lord, you are slow, for shame, away.*
King: *Can we outrun the heavens? Good Margaret stay.*
Queen: *What are you made of? You'll nor fight nor fly:*
*Now is it manhood, wisdom, and defense,*
*To give the enemy way, and to secure us*
*By what we can, which can no more but fly.* (V, ii, 72–77)

When Margaret's forces gain the advantage and win, one of her captains, Clifford, captures the Duke of York's youngest son, the child Rutland. Taking a scene from historian Holinshed's account of the battle, Shakespeare adds Margaret as the active leader in the capture of York. By Margaret's orders Richard is placed on a molehill and crowned with a paper crown. Margaret hands him a handkerchief stained with the blood of his son Rutland:

*Look York, I stained this napkin with the blood*
*That valiant Clifford, with his rapier's point,*
*Made issue from the bosom of the boy:*
*And if thine eyes can water for his death,*
*I give thee this to dry thy cheeks withal.* (Part 3, I, iv, 79–83)

In assuming the leadership and the strategy of battle, Margaret has taken on its worst qualities, the cruelty and the bloodthirstiness of the kill. Now she taunts Richard of York: "I, to make thee mad, do mock thee thus. / Stamp, rave, and fret, that I may sing and dance" (90–91). Peggy Ashcroft, with a

French accent as Margaret in the Royal Shakespeare Company 1964 production, produced a chilling effect as she sang and danced at this point. While hardened warrior Northumberland weeps for York's plight, Clifford and Margaret stab him to death.

The Yorks finally win, the son of the Duke of York becomes King Richard III, and in the play of that name, Margaret appears as an aged, dethroned queen. Bereft of political and physical power, she resorts to verbal attacks. Her speech shifts again into a prophet's warning of disasters to befall the Yorks in retribution for their wrongs. Her curses and prophecies, as they come to pass, become the framework for the action of the play and contribute to the defeat of Richard III.

*Troilus and Cressida*—Cressida

In many ways, Cressida is a woman locked in a legend. By the time of Shakespeare's satirical comedy or "comicall satyre" as O. J. Campbell defines it,[1] her name *was* legend, a by-word for infidelity because she betrays her oath to Troilus. She repeats in the play the vow for which she was famous (or infamous):

> *Oh you gods divine,*
> *Make Cressid's name the very crown of falsehood,*
> *If ever she leave Troilus.* (IV, ii, 100-102)

In Shakespeare's source, Chaucer's *Troilus and Criseyde,* she is described as "slydinge of corage," changeable in heart, inconstant. Scottish poet Robert Henryson, whose version also was popular, punishes Cressida's infidelity by depicting her at the end as a leprous beggar. Pistol so refers to Doll in *King Henry V* as a "lazar kite of Cressid's kind" (II, i, 78). Although Shakespeare follows the legendary story line, his characterization of Cressida is more sympathetic. No longer is she the older partner, a widow wise to the ways of the world, as in Chaucer. As the action begins, she and Troilus are both young and genuinely in love with each other.

Shakespeare always favored a double plot, and his version of the story incorporates events of the Trojan War prior to and including the death of Hector. The war plot, which parallels the love story, depicts Greek and Trojan warriors familiar to the audience through history and literature like Homer's *Iliad,* which had been translated by Shakespeare's contemporary,

George Chapman. In the classical account, Troilus is mentioned in passing, and there is no love story. Yet by Shakespeare's day, the legend of Troilus and Cressida was a by-word. Rosalind in *As You Like It* refers to Troilus in reminding Orlando that no man ever died for love:

> *Troilus had his brains dashed out with a Grecian club, yet he did what he could to die before, and he is one of the patterns of love.* (IV, i, 92–94)

The medieval flavor of Chaucer's story persists in Shakespeare, as a Greek or Trojan warrior is referred to as a "knight" and his loved one as his "lady." When Greek Diomedes captures Troilus's horse in battle, he sends it to Cressida in Shakespeare's version as in he did in Chaucer's:

> *Go, go, my servant, take thou Troilus' horse.*
> *Present the fair steed to my lady Cressid,*
> *Fellow, commend my service to her beauty:*
> *Tell her I have chastised the amorous Trojan,*
> *And am her knight by proof.* (V, v, 1–5)

Having inherited a legendary Cressida, Shakespeare attempts to motivate her desertion of Troilus by depicting her as a realist who must adapt to the situation in which she finds herself, no matter how dangerous or distasteful. Troilus remains, as in Chaucer, a moonstruck courtly lover divorced from reality. Pandarus, a humorous character in Chaucer, is more cynical in the play and somewhat sinister. His counterpart in cynicism is the Greek Thersites, whose waspish commentary satirizes courtly love as well as the *Iliad*'s glorification of war.

As he enters the play with Pandarus, who seems always to be hanging over the pair, Troilus displays all the symptoms of courtly love in his unrequited devotion to Cressida—he declares his suffering rhetorically and describes his lady as a nonpareil. Cressida appears like a breath of fresh air, clearly seeing Pandarus for what he is (a pander) and cleverly retorting to his sexual innuendo with some of her own. She pertly picks up his metaphor, his words, and his rhythm to deflate and ridicule his overpraising of Troilus:

> Pandarus: *He will weep you an 'twere a man born in April.*
> Cressida: *And I'll spring up in his tears an 'twere a nettle against May.* (I, ii, 168-71)

In a soliloquy—a device rarely used in the comedies to reveal serious introspection—she questions why she continues to "hold off" when she does love Troilus, in whom she sees more than a "thousandfold" of virtues. "Men prize the thing ungained more than it is," she decides, and offers advice to the women in the audience: "Therefore this maxim out of love I teach: / 'Achievement is command; ungained, beseech'" (I, ii, 283–84). As Chaucer's Criseyde says, "I am myn owene womman" (Book I, 750). Philip Edwards points out, "there is something truer in Cressida than he [Troilus] recognized, though alas it did not express itself in constancy. Her worldly prudence in not showing her affection for Troilus too quickly is a wisdom she has acquired from many sources in Shakespeare and elsewhere. . . . She may have been right, even about Troilus, who protests too much."[2] Cressida fears that if she makes known her love to Troilus, he will dominate ("command") her.

Surrounded by men throughout the play, Cressida is a lonely woman who must be her own defense. She has no confidant, Troilus fails to actively support her, and her father, who in Chaucer's version welcomes her to the Greek camp, is absent in the play when she arrives there and is humiliated by the Greeks. Ironically, in the end she is dominated not as she feared, by Troilus, who loves her, but by Diomedes, who will subjugate her.

Although she decided earlier to "hold off," when Pandarus finally brings the two together, she confesses her love, signaling her later change of mind:

> *Prince Troilus, I have loved you night and day*
> *For many weary months.*
> Troilus: *Why was my Cressid then so hard to win? . . .*
> Cressida: *If I confess much, you will play the tyrant.*
> (III, ii, 111–15)

Faced with the problem of sympathetically presenting a woman whose bad reputation was legendary, Shakespeare uses Pandarus to detract from implications of romance in the meeting of Troilus and Cressida and in their expressions of love. Having brought the two together, Pandarus oversees and comments on their meeting for a night of love: "Come, draw this curtain, and let's see your picture" (urging them to disrobe). "So so, rub on and kiss the mistress: how now, a kiss in fee farm?"[i]

[i] absolute possession

In the lovers' first-meeting dialogue Cressida expresses her fear:

> Troilus: *What too curious dreg espies my lady in the fountain of our love?*
> Cressida: *More dregs than water, if my fears have eyes. . . . Blind fear, that seeing reason leads, finds safer footing than blind reason stumbling without fear. To fear the worst, oft cures the worse.* (III, ii, 63–70)

Chaucer spins out their alliance for three years, but Shakespeare gives them only one night together. Her parting from Troilus results from the constant demands of her father (a Trojan deserter now in the Greek camp) that the Trojans release his daughter. The release is secured by a Greek exchange of a captured Trojan. When the lovers part, they pledge eternal fidelity, Troilus vowing that "True swains in love shall in the world to come / Approve[i] their truths by Troilus." Cressida swears,

> *If I be false, or swerve a hair from truth,*
> *When Time is old, or hath forgot itself,*
> *When water drops have worn the stones of Troy,*
> *And blind oblivion swallowed cities up. . . .*
> *yet let memory,*
> *From false to false, among false maids in love,*
> *Upbraid my falsehood, when th' have said 'as false*
> *As air, as water, wind or sandy earth'. . .*
> *Yet let them say, to stick the heart of falsehood,*
> *'As false as Cressid.'* (III, ii, 168-69, 179-91)

Cynical comments throughout the play by Pandarus, Thersites, and others tinge both the love story and the feats of war, in which the heroes are less than heroic. Tired of war, the men of both sides debate whether the cause was worth it—Trojan Paris's abduction of Helen from her Greek husband, Menelaus. Hector, the hero of the Trojan side, argues, "Let Helen go":

> *If we have lost so many tenths of ours,*
> *To guard a thing not ours nor worth to us*

[i] prove

*(Had it our name) the value of one tenth,*
*What merit's in that reason which denies*
*The yielding of her up?* (II, ii, 17, 21–25)

But the romantics, Paris and Troilus, prevail, and the war goes on.

There is only one scene between Paris and Helen and that is not a love scene but one of sexual banter with Pandarus. He has come to ask Paris to make excuses for the absence of Troilus, who has gone to a love tryst with Cressida. It is clear that Paris is bedazzled by Helen; he is supposed to be fighting the Greeks along with the other Trojan warriors, but Helen keeps him from the field: "I would fain have armed today, but my Nell would not have it so" (III, i, 131). Pandarus offers to sing a song, and Helen remarks, "Let thy song be love. This love will undo us all. O Cupid, Cupid, Cupid" (104-105). Pandarus's song begins "Love, love, nothing but love, still love, still more," and concludes with bawdy innuendo. Later in the action, when Diomedes arrives in Troy to accompany Cressida to the Greek camp, Paris asks whether he or Menelaus deserves "fair Helen" best. Diomedes replies, "Both alike":

*He, like a puling cuckold, would drink up*
*The lees and dregs of a flat tame'd piece:*
*You, like a lecher, out of whorish loins*
*Are pleased to breed out your inheritors.* (IV, i, 63–66)

Once Cressida arrives at the Greek camp (IV, v), she is again a woman alone among men and must undergo the indignity of being passed from hand to hand among them. In the play's atmosphere of cynicism, Ulysses's comments about Cressida among the Greek warriors might be regarded as wishful thinking rather than as fact. One might compare Iago's remarks to Roderigo, interpreting Desdemona's behavior with Cassio as "lechery" and "paddling with the palm of his hand," which Roderigo claims "was but courtesy"(II, i, 254–55). As each of the Greeks attempts to kiss Cressida, Ulysses comments, "There's language in her eye, her cheek, her lip," and pronounces her one of the "daughters of the game," but when some of the men ask for a kiss, she denies them. As nothing in the text bears out Ulysses's remarks, only in the direction and performance can it be seen whether he is truthful or, like Iago, offering a denigrating interpretation for his own ends. For today's audiences, the latter seems more acceptable, with a frightened Cressida meeting a threatening situation, as Shakespeare's heroines often do, with resourcefulness aimed at self-protection. In the 1999 production at the Royal National Theatre, directed by Trevor Nunn, Cressida resigns to the situation and adapts her behavior to meet it.

Cressida's final scene (act five, scene two) is original with Shakespeare. She is alone with Diomedes in an encounter observed by Troilus and Ulysses. Despite the comments of the unseen two who are eavesdropping, joined by Thersites, her actions may be interpreted as desperation on her part as she attempts to defend herself against an onslaught by boorish Diomedes. She may be flirtatious and changeable—giving him a token that Troilus had presented to her as a symbol of his undying love—but it must be noted that she does not succumb. How long she can or will hold off is enigmatic, for when Diomedes bluntly states, "I do not like this fooling," she invites him to return (108).

Earlier, Cressida had warned Troilus that she had "a kind of self resides with you," which now prompts his refusal to believe what he is seeing, as he remarks: "This is, and is not, Cressid." Philip Edwards notes that Troilus "never really sees Cressida but has a cloudy vision of a blessed damozel. He has little right, when he discovers Cressida and Diomedes together, to exclaim so vehemently that the 'bonds of heaven' have been 'unloosed.' His disillusionment is the puncturing of a self-inflated world."[3]

In her final soliloquy, Cressida accepts the situation, recognizing that hers is a mind "swayed by eyes": "What error leads must err: O then conclude, / 'Minds swayed by eyes are full of turpitude'" (V, ii, 117–18). Shakespeare cannot change legend, but he has created a new perspective on that legend, deepening the characterization of a heroine trapped by circumstance. "Betrayal is the governing concept of the play," in Cressida's fall as in Hector's, notes Barbara Everett.[4] Like the warriors on the field whose struggle parallels her own love affair, Cressida is defeated in a battle that in Shakespeare's account is somewhat tarnished.

*Antony and Cleopatra*—Cleopatra

While Romeo and Juliet personify young love, Antony and Cleopatra are Shakespeare's tribute to mature love. When Shakespeare wrote his play, the middle-aged pair were already legendary, immortalized by ancient historians, including Plutarch, whose account North translated into the English version used by Shakespeare as his source.

A combination of sex, high drama, politics, and war, the action is dominated by this larger-than-life couple whose love is of a magnitude as great as their positions of power in the world. He is one of the triumvirate, the three who ruled the Roman empire from its western capital, Rome. She is queen of Egypt, the fertile, mysterious East. Mutuality is the secret of the successful love of this "mutual pair," although their love at times is as turbulent as the politics. The entire play might be considered as metaphor, a favorite one of the sonneteers—love versus war and a variation, love as war. The love of Cleopatra and Antony is fulfilling and productive, as opposed to the destruction of war. It is a reciprocal relationship that is never static and always inventive, often accusatory, and sometimes jealous and deceptive. But as Rosalie Colie observes, "the simplicity, single-heartedness and intensity of this faulty human love . . . comes to seem a far greater achievement than the Roman quest for power."[5]

As the play opens, the Roman soldiers may complain that Antony has deserted the manly art of war "and is become the bellows and the fan / To cool a gipsy's[i] lust," but when he enters with Cleopatra, the impression of their love is one of magnificence. It is an impression created entirely through the poetry; as has been noted many times, there is little physicality depicted after an initial kiss or embrace at Antony's declaration:

*Let Rome in Tiber melt, and the wide arch*
*Of the ranged empire fall: . . . the nobleness of life*
*Is to do thus: when such a mutual pair,*
*And such a twain can do't, in which I bind*
*On pain of punishment, the world to weet*[ii]
*We stand up peerless.* (I, i, 34–41)

[i] Egyptian's [ii] know

The poetry on the grand scale is consistent with the pair and their love. John Holloway sees not only their mutual nobility as characterizing the bond between Antony and Cleopatra but also their "intense and exuberant physical energy" that issues "from sexuality itself in the full tide of its fulfillment."[6]

Cleopatra's "infinite variety" might be considered a handbook on how to keep a lover intrigued and enraptured. One approach is never to let him off the hook. In their first appearance, after his high-soaring poetic description of their love, she deflates it as an "excellent falsehood" and reminds him that he is married to Fulvia. His response is that even Cleopatra's "chiding" becomes her, as do her laughter and tears. When Antony is absent, Charmian is instructed by Cleopatra to seek him and report her mood as the opposite of his:

*See where he is, who's with him, what he does:*
*I did not send you: if you find him sad,*
*Say I am dancing: if in mirth, report*
*That I am sudden sick: quick, and return.* (I, iii, 3–6)

Harley Granville-Barker, a notable stage director as well as a scholar, comments on this passage, "here is actuality; and forged in words of one syllable, mainly. This is the woman herself, quick, jealous, imperious, mischievous, malicious, flagrant, subtle . . . and the light, glib verse seems to set her on tiptoe."[7] When Charmian suggests the way to hold him is "In each thing give him way / Cross him in nothing," Cleopatra shrewdly responds: "Thou teachest like a fool: the way to lose him" (I, iii, 9–10). Her vivacity and unpredictability keep him off balance and dependent on her to recover that balance. If Antony is losing his identity as a warrior, he is finding his identity as a man with Cleopatra.

Not only is there "infinite variety" in her moods and actions, but her language also is varied in its rhythms, imagery, and vocabulary. In her speech she may be fragmentary and colloquial or lofty and poetic. When Antony insists that he must leave for Rome because the state is in danger from Pompey and that she need not fear releasing him because Fulvia is dead, she taunts his lack of emotion and predicts he will greet her death the same way:

*O most false love!*
*Where be the sacred vials thou should'st fill*
*With sorrowful water? Now I see, I see*
*In Fulvia's death how mine received shall be.* (I, iii, 63–66)

The repetition of the "s" sound almost hisses at him, as she continues to bate him on his "dissembling" and to interrupt his attempts at explaining, until he bluntly states, "I'll leave you, lady." Her reply is completely opposite to her earlier taunts; it is simple and fragmented:

*Sir, you and I must part, but that's not it;*
*Sir, you and I have loved, but there's not it;*
*That you know well, something it is I would—*
*O my oblivion*[i] *is a very Antony*
*And I am all forgotten.* (I, iii, 87–93)

Cleopatra's allusions and metaphors often combine physical love-making with the grandeur of the elements, as in her reply when Octavius's messenger asks to kiss her hand:

*Your Caesar's father oft,*
*When he hath mused of taking kingdoms in,*
*Bestowed his lips on that unworthy place,*
*As it rained kisses.* (III, xiii, 82–85)

Cleopatra's dream of an "Emperor Antony" after his death is expressed in a series of images that evoke the magnificence of the man and their love. All the elements, the seasons, the world, and the universe itself combine in her tribute to him in terms she would never utter to him during his lifetime for fear of relinquishing her power over him:

*His face was as the heavens, and therein stuck*
*A sun and moon which kept their course and lighted*
*The little O, the earth. . . .*
*His legs bestrid the ocean, his rear'ed arm*
*Crested the world: his voice was propertied*[ii]
*As all the tun'ed*[iii] *spheres, and that to friends:*
*But when he meant to quail and shake the orb,*
*He was as rattling thunder. For his bounty,*
*There was no winter in't: an autumn 'twas*
*That grew the more by reaping: his delights*
*Were dolphin-like, they showed his back above*

[i] forgetfulness, like his in forgetting her [ii] as musical [iii] music-making

*The element they lived in.* (V, ii, 78-89)

When Antony is dying, Cleopatra invokes the elements in images that describe an alteration in the world itself. As the sun, like Antony, disappears, the world is left dark:

*O sun,*
*Burn the great sphere thou movest in, darkling stand*
*The varying shore o'th' world.* (IV, xv, 10–12)

After Antony's death, Cleopatra continues the imagery of a changed world, introducing the people of the world and progressing down the scale from Antony as "the garland of the war," to his soldiers and their implements, now in disuse, and finally to children, "level now with men" because with Antony gone, "there is nothing left remarkable" with which to make comparisons:

*O withered is the garland of the war,*
*The soldier's pole is fall'n. Young boys and girls*
*Are level now with men, the odds is gone,*
*And there is nothing left remarkable*
*Beneath the visiting moon.* (IV, xv, 66-70)

The account of Cleopatra's first meeting with Antony is another passage, like her "emperor" tribute, in which images and allusions envelop a person to create an effect of sensual magnificence. Even Antony's rugged soldier Enobarbus, who sees through Cleopatra's wiles, praises her as he describes her to the Romans, the passage closely following its source in North. She dramatized herself, appearing like Venus, the goddess of love, attended by nymphs on a perfumed barge and, declining his invitation to dine, asked him to dine with her in her own sumptuous setting.[8] Enobarbus concludes:

*Age cannot wither her, nor custom stale*
*Her infinite variety: other women cloy*
*The appetites they feed, but she makes hungry*
*Where most she satisfies.* (II, ii, 245-48)

She takes delight in their love-making, as implied by Enobarbus and made explicit when, in Anthony's absence, she envies his horse: "O happy horse to bear the weight of Antony!" (I, v, 22). She never lets him forget her when he is absent, and sends him messages daily. She flaunts her sexuality, nor does she confine it to Antony, who almost kills a messenger whom she grants her hand to be kissed. Enobarbus reports that "The holy priests / Bless her, when she is riggish."[i] (II, ii, 249-50). She is as jealous as Antony is, but she is not defeated when she hears of his marriage to Octavia. Recovering from her initial shock, she transforms every reported physical attribute, except age, into an advantage for her and a detriment for the new wife. She is inventive in their joyous dealings with each other, playing a practical trick of hanging a salt fish on his fishing hook. They will, in disguise, "wander through the streets, / And note the qualities of people" (I, i, 54). And in an intimate moment she describes, she puts her "tires"[ii] on him and she wears his sword.

Self-dramatizing, she presents herself as goddesses, appearing as the Roman Venus when she and Antony meet, and as the Egyptian Isis in the marketplace with her sons to announce Egypt's newly acquired lands, courtesy of Antony. And she stages her death. She knows when to exaggerate her love and when to state it simply, as in their parting in act one, scene three. If a lie will serve her turn, she will use it, although "Cleopatra's is a consistent and therefore honest duplicity, compared to Octavius's slyness."[9] Her worst deception is to send Antony news of her death to assuage his anger at her desertion of the battlefield, at which news he attempts suicide and later dies in her arms.

"The preoccupation with sex and with the shared sexuality of Antony and Cleopatra runs as an undercurrent through the play," notes Colie. "The emotions shared by them challenge the heroic world of the Roman military organization."[10] Politically, it is Antony's marriages that contribute to his wars with Octavius. From act three, scene seven on, the action is increasingly concerned with the war between Antony and Octavius Caesar for control of the Roman empire. Fulvia, Antony's first wife, is reported to have warred against Octavius in order to draw her husband back to Rome and away from Cleopatra. After Fulvia's death Antony marries Octavia, the sister of Octavius, to cement relations between the two men. But when Antony returns to Cleopatra, Octavius, outraged at the betrayal of his sister, launches full-scale war against Antony. The emphasis on love as

[i] sexy [ii] attire

well as on war is what differentiates this play from Shakespeare's other Roman tragedies, like *Julius Caesar* and *Coriolanus.*

As queen of Egypt, Cleopatra is a good politician who, through Antony's generosity and her hold over him, acquires entire kingdoms for annexation to her country. Antony "made her / Of Lower Syria, Cyprus, Lydia, / Absolute queen"—and she gains additional lands for her sons and brother (III, vi, 9–11). Her lack of experience in warfare does not deter her from insisting to Enobarbus, who argues against her participation, that she will lead her own forces:

> *A charge*[i] *we bear i'th' war,*
> *And as the president of my kingdom will*
> *Appear there for*[ii] *a man. Speak not against it,*
> *I will not stay behind.* (III, vii, 16–19)

She insists they fight by sea; against Enobarbus's advice, Antony agrees. When she decides to take her ships and flee the battle, he follows, and they lose. He feels betrayed by her, but Cleopatra, all abject apology, wins his pardon, as he declares, drawing his imagery from ships:

> *Egypt, thou knew'st too well,*
> *My heart was to thy rudder tied by th' strings,*
> *And thou shouldst tow me after.* (III, xi, 56–58)

Antony challenges Octavius to single combat, but the younger man, having superior troops, declines. In the morning, although the outcome of the day's battle is uncertain, Cleopatra delights in helping Eros deck Antony in his armor, a stage picture suggesting the paintings of Venus arming Mars.

As Antony goes off to battle, realist Cleopatra voices her doubts of his success:

> *He goes forth gallantly. That he and Caesar might*
> *Determine this great war in single fight—*
> *Then Antony—but now—Well, on.* (IV, iv, 36–38)

But Antony wins the day and "returns his victory to her"; exclaiming, "leap thou, attire and all / Through proof of harness to my heart, and there / Ride on the pants triumphing" (IV, viii,

[i] expense [ii] as

14–16). He has won a victory over the legions of Octavius, but she has conquered Antony.

The contrast between Rome and Egypt is apparent throughout, between the tough Roman soldiers and the two women and a eunuch who are the attendants of Cleopatra; in the settings, the austerity of Rome and the opulence of Egypt; and in the imagery. Characterizing Cleopatra and Egypt are her images of fecundity. As she parts from Antony, who accuses her of "idleness,"[i] Cleopatra responds with an image from childbirth to describe her suffering at his absence: "'Tis sweating labor / To bear such idleness so near the heart" (I, iii, 95–96). When Antony is enraged at her flirting with a messenger from Octavius, and asks, "To flatter Caesar, would you mingle eyes / With one that ties his points?",[ii] she testifies to the sincerity of her love. She invokes poisoned hail to kill her, Caesarian (her son by Julius Caesar), and all her other children, "the memory of my womb." Should she prove unfaithful, her children should "graveless," be eaten by flies and gnats of the Nile. The Nile itself, often alluded to, is a symbol of fruitfulness.

The most telling and also the most simple of all Cleopatra's fecundity images is her description of the asp, the poisonous snake whose bite is death, at her breast as she dies in her robes of state, upon her throne, addressing Antony, now that he is dead, as "husband": "Dost thou not see my baby at my breast, / That sucks the nurse asleep?" (V, ii, 308–9).

The problem with most productions of the play is that Cleopatra as a character is much more vivid than Antony. Taken line for line, she has almost all the best dialogue. In addition to his initial speech, Antony has one superb passage (IV, xiv, 2–10) about the "rack" or cloud, which "dislimns," or fades, a metaphor of his loss of selfhood, which is a subtheme of the play. Memorable stage Cleopatras include Vanessa Redgrave and most recently, Helen Mirren, while Jane LaPotaire is impressive in the 1980 BBC Time-Life television presentation. The problem with the last named is that Antony, played by Colin Blakely, offers an interpretation that is hardly "noble," the adjective by which he is addressed and described in the play. It is difficult to fathom what the vibrant Cleopatra of LaPotaire could possibly

[i] trifling [ii] laces

see in this dull Antony. Most heroic was Anthony Hopkins matched by an equally heroic Judi Dench as Cleopatra in 1987 on the stage of London's Royal National Theatre. Theirs was the last of the performances of these roles in which the lines were delivered at full voice, and the action was on the grand scale.

Perhaps the world of the stage has shrunk since then, along with the world itself. A production for the current times, at that same theater in the autumn of 1998, was the *Antony and Cleopatra* with Alan Rickman and Helen Mirren in the leading roles. What it lost in "rattling thunder" it made up for in subtlety. Rickman was the most subtly varied of Antonys, as might be expected of this actor, an Antony for the modern stage as it were, vestiges of his former nobility still discernible but visibly searching for his lost identity. Mirren was the definitive Cleopatra for these times, sexually vibrant and brilliantly portraying all the "infinite variety" of the character's aspects and moods. Samuel West must be mentioned for his Octavius; it is rare for an actor in that role to show any subtlety at all, but West, facing the audience when Octavius is brought news of Antony's death in act five, scene one, displayed a sensitivity worthy of Hamlet.

While all the other memorable heroines Shakespeare portrays are unique in their characterization and their dialogue, Cleopatra, justifying her share of the play's title, is unforgettable as the most mature and the most alluring of his women in love.

## Notes

[1] Oscar James Campbell, *Comicall Satyre and 'Troilus and Cressida'*.

[2] Philip Edwards, *Shakespeare: A Writer's Progress*, 129.

[3] Ibid.

[4] Barbara Everett, *Young Hamlet*, 173.

[5] Rosalie Cole, *Shakespeare's Living Art*, 194.

[6] John Holloway, *The Story of the Night*, 105.

[7] Harley Granville-Barker, *Prefaces to Shakespeare*, III, 72.

[8] Alice Griffin, *Sources of Ten Shakespearean Plays*, 268–69.

[9] Colie, *Living Art*, 182.

[10] Ibid., 186.

# BIBLIOGRAPHY

Adelman, Janet. *Suffocating Mothers: Fantasies of Maternal Origin in Shakespeare's Plays.* New York: Routledge, 1992.

Barber, C. L. *Shakespeare's Festive Comedy.* Princeton: Princeton University Press, 1972.

Barton, Anne. *Essays, Mainly Shakespearean.* Cambridge: Cambridge University Press, 1994.

———. "Love's Labours Lost." In *Shakespeare: Early Comedies.* Edited by Pamela Mason, 197–220. London: Macmillan, 1995.

———. "The Taming of the Shrew." *The Riverside Shakespeare.* New York: 1974. 106–109.

Bradbrook, Muriel C. "London Pageantry and Lawyers' Theater." In *Shakespeare's Rough Magic.* Edited by Peter Erickson and Coppelia Kahn, 256–68. Newark, Del.: University of Delaware Press, 1985.

———. *Shakespeare: The Poet in his World.* London: Methuen, 1980.

Bradley, A. C. *Shakespearean Tragedy.* 1904; New York: Viking Penguin, 1991.

Brooks, Cleanth. *The Well Wrought Urn.* 1949; New York: Harbrace, 1956.

Campbell, Oscar J. *Comicall Satyre and 'Troilus and Cressida.'* San Marino, Cal.: Huntington Library Publications, 1938.

Charnes, Linda. *Notorious Identity: Materializing the Subject in Shakespeare.* Cambridge, Mass.: Harvard University Press, 1993.

Colie, Rosalie L. *Shakespeare's Living Art.* Princeton: Princeton University Press, 1974.

Cook, Carol. "The Fatal Cleopatra." In *Shakespearean Tragedy and Gender.* Edited by Shirley Nelson Garner and Madelon

Sprengnether, 241–67. Bloomington, Ind.: Indiana University Press: 1996.

Crawford, John W. *The Learning, Wit, and Wisdom of Shakespeare's Women.* Lewiston, N.Y.: Edwin Mellen Press, 1997.

Daniell, David. "The Good Marriage of Katherine and Petruchio." In *Shakespeare: Early Comedies.* Edited by Pamela Mason, 121–37. London: Macmillan, 1995.

Dusinberre, Juliet. *Shakespeare and the Nature of Woman*, 2d ed. New York: St. Martin's Press, 1996.

Edwards, Philip. *Shakespeare: A Writer's Progress.* New York: Oxford University Press, 1986.

Erickson, Peter. *Patriarchal Structures in Shakespeare's Dramas.* Berkeley: University of California Press, 1985.

Everett, Barbara. "Introduction." In *All's Well that Ends Well.* Edited by Barbara Everett, 7–42. New York: Penguin Books, 1970.

———. *"Much Ado About Nothing." Critical Quarterly* 3, 4 (winter 1961), 319–35.

———. *Young Hamlet: Essays on Shakespeare's Tragedies.* 1989; New York: Oxford University Press, 1990.

Gardner, Helen. *"As You Like It."* In *Shakespeare: The Comedies.* Edited by Kenneth Muir, 58–71. Englewood Cliffs, N.J.: Prentice-Hall, 1965.

Gay, Penny. *As She Likes It: Shakespeare's Unruly Women.* New York: Routledge, 1994.

Granville-Barker, Harley. *Prefaces to Shakespeare*, vols. 2, 3. Princeton: Princeton University Press, 1946.

Griffin, Alice. *Pageantry on the Shakespearean Stage.* 1952; New Haven, Conn.: College and University Press, 1975.

———. *Rebels and Lovers: Shakespeare's Young Heroes and Heroines.* New York: New York University Press, 1976.

———. *The Sources of Ten Shakespearean Plays.* New York: Thomas Y. Crowell, 1966.

Harbage, Alfred. *Shakespeare's Audience.* New York: Columbia University Press, 1941.

Heilman, Robert B. *Magic in the Web: Action and Language in "Othello".* Lexington: University of Kentucky Press, 1956.

Holloway, John. *The Story of the Night.* Lincoln: University of Nebraska Press, 1961.

Honigmann, E. A. J. *Myriad-Minded Shakespeare.* New York: Macmillan, 1989.

Kahn, Coppelia. "The Cuckoo's Note: Male Friendship and Cuckoldry in *The Merchant of Venice.*" In *Shakespeare's Comedies.* Edited by Gary Waller, 128–37. London: Longman, 1991.

———. *Man's Estate: Masculine Identity in Shakespeare.* Berkeley: University of California Press, 1981.

Leavis, F. R. *The Common Pursuit*. London: Chatto & Windus, 1952.

Leverenz, David. "The Woman in Hamlet: An Interpersonal View." In *Representing Shakespeare: New Psychoanalytic Essays.* Edited by Murray M. Schwartz and Coppelia Kahn, 110–28. Baltimore: Johns Hopkins University Press, 1980.

Lodge, Thomas. *Rosalind.* In *Elizabethan Prose Fiction,* edited by Merritt Lawlis, 278–394. New York: Odyssey Press, 1967.

Lothian, J. M. and T.W. Craik, eds. *Twelfth Night*. Arden ed. New York: Methuen, 1975.

McKewin, Carole. "Counsels of Gall and Grace: Intimate Conversations between Women in Shakespeare's Plays." In *The Woman's Part: Feminist Criticism of Shakespeare.* Edited by Carolyn Lenz, Gayle Greene, and Carol Thomas Neely, 117–31. Urbana: University of Illinois Press, 1983.

Mason, Pamela, ed. *Shakespeare: Early Comedies.* London: Macmillan, 1995.

Mortimer, Penelope. "*The Taming of the Shrew.*" In *Shakespeare in Perspective* , vol. 1. Edited by Roger Sales, 197–98. London: Ariel Books, 1982.

Muir, Kenneth, ed. *Macbeth.* Arden ed. New York: Methuen, 1964.

Neely, Carol Thomas. *Broken Nuptials in Shakespeare's Plays.* New Haven, Conn.: Yale University Press, 1985.

———. "Women and Men in *Othello.*" In *The Woman's Part: Feminist Criticism of Shakespeare.* Edited by Carolyn Lenz, Gayle Greene, and Carol Thomas Neely, 211–39. Urbana: University of Illinois Press, 1983.

Novy, Marianne. *Love's Argument: Gender Relations in Shakespeare.* Chapel Hill, N.C.: University of North Carolina Press, 1984.

Rutter, Carol. *Clamorous Voices: Shakespeare's Women Today.* New York: Routledge, 1989.

Scales, Prunella. "*The Merry Wives of Windsor*." In *Shakespeare in Perspective,* vol. 2. Edited by Roger Sales, 142–49. London: Ariel Books, 1985.

Shaw, George Bernard. *Shaw on Shakespeare*. Edited by Edwin Wilson. New York: E. P. Dutton, 1961.

Suzman, Janet. "*As You Like It*." In *Shakespeare in Perspective,* vol. 1. Edited by Roger Sales, 56–58. London: Ariel Books, 1982.

Van Doren, Mark. *Shakespeare: Five Great Tragedies.* New York: Pocket Books, 1939.

Webster, Margaret. *Shakespeare Without Tears*. 1942; New York: World Publishing, 1955.

Weiss, Theodore. *The Breath of Clowns and Kings: Shakespeare's Early Comedies and Histories.* London: Chatto & Windus, 1971.

# ABOUT THE AUTHOR

Alice Griffin is professor emerita of English at Hunter and Lehman Colleges, The City University of New York. She is the author of *Pageantry on the Shakespearean Stage* (Twayne, 1952; College and Univ. Press, 1975), *The Sources of Ten Shakespearean Plays* (Thomas Y. Crowell, 1966), and *Rebels and Lovers: Shakespeare's Young Heroes and Heroines* (New York University Press, 1976). She has reviewed stage and film productions of Shakespeare in *The Shakespeare Quarterly, Theatre Arts Magazine,* and *Variety* and on radio station WNYC in New York. Her books on theater include *Living Theatre* (Twayne, 1954), *Understanding Tennessee Williams* (University of South Carolina Press, 1995), *Understanding Arthur Miller* (University of South Carolina Press, 1996) and *Understanding Lillian Hellman* (University of South Carolina Press, 1999). Her monthly website on drama, *theaterpro.com,* includes a section on Shakespeare.

# INDEX

ERRATA: Any page annotation after 53 will be found two pages prior to the page number listed in the index.

*(i.e., an annotation listing a reference page of 127 will actually be found on page 125.)*

## A



## B

## C

## D

## G



## H

## M



## N

## O



## P

## Q



## R

## S



## T